Commission To Every Nation

Commission To Every Nation

HOW PEOPLE JUST LIKE YOU ARE BLESSING THE NATIONS

■ ■ ■

Richard Malm

Printed in the United States of America
First Printing, 2017
ISBN-13: 9780998508597
ISBN-10: 0998508594

Thanks to:
    Editing: Carol Jones
                    Benchmark Creative Resources
    Cover: Joe Cavazos Design
    Copywriting: Anna McKenzie

ORE Publishing
Texas

Author Contact:
Richard Malm
P.O. Box 291002
Kerrville, TX 78029-1002
RickMalm@cten.org

His ways are higher
than your ways.
His thoughts are higher
than your thoughts.
Is it possible
His dreams for you
are higher
Than your dreams
for yourself?

~ RM

In Appreciation

■ ■ ■

THANK YOU, JANA, FOR BEING such a faithful traveling companion on this continuing Divine Adventure. Neither of us imagined the places it would take us and the things we would experience when we started down this road. We just knew we wanted to follow the Lord wherever He led.

It's been fun. It's been exciting. But there have also been dark valleys and dry deserts. I'm so thankful I had you by my side to share the joys and sorrows as we journeyed together with Him.

I also want to thank all those who have partnered with our ministry to make this amazing experiment possible. Some of you were with us from the very beginning. We were privileged to meet some of you along the way. We treasure your friendship, prayers, encouragement, and the financial investments you've made throughout the years. As you've sown into our lives, you've enabled this dream, which has enabled thousands of others to serve millions around the globe.

Finally, thank you to all the current and former CTEN staff and missionaries. Your servant hearts have made CTEN much more than an organization. You've made it an organism, a living family. May it always be a community of brothers and sisters loving, laughing, and serving together to bring a smile to the face of our Father.

Table of Contents

It's Not Right Or Wrong, Just Different

■ ■ ■

I'VE BEEN HELD AT GUNPOINT twice, had a knife put to my throat, been surrounded by angry mobs, and faced other life and death situations. I've even been threatened with an IRS audit by a furious agent. But by far, the most terrifying experience of my life was driving in England. As everyone knows, the British drive on the wrong side of the road. And the steering wheel is on the wrong side of the car. And the car had a manual transmission, so I had to shift with the wrong hand.

Driving there was terrifying; but there's nothing right or wrong with British cars or British driving patterns. They're just different than what I'm used to. One of the most important things a missionary learns when ministering in another culture is that different isn't necessarily right or wrong - it's just different.

This is the story of a different way to do missions. In this book, I explain why we do things the way we do at Commission To Every Nation (or CTEN, pronounced: see TEN) and how our methods naturally emerged. Because we do things differently, it would be easy to assume I'm saying others do it wrong - especially since I'm passionate about the way we do it.

The truth is I have a profound respect for all the great mission organizations that do it differently than we do. A hammer and a screwdriver are totally different because they have different functions. Churches and mission agencies are like that. Each was forged by the Master to accomplish a different job.

Tools even come in different sizes. As impressive as my huge wrench might be, it's totally useless when I'm working in a small space. God uses various tools, with various designs and various sizes, but every tool - like every individual - was designed to accomplish a specific purpose and functions most effectively when doing what it was designed to do, the way it was designed to do it.

"For we are God's masterpiece. He has created us anew in Christ Jesus, so we can do the good things He planned for us long ago."[1]

Jesus told us what to do - Go and make disciples. He didn't say how to do it. That has resulted in countless methods. Some drive on the right side of the road, some on the left side. Some go right down the middle and some avoid roads all together. It's not how we get there that matters, but that we all keep moving toward the goal - encouraging, supporting, and cheering for one another along the way.[2]

YOUR NAME BELONGS IN HIS-STORY

This is a story about how God surprised some very ordinary people and did some extraordinary things through them. Some of the names have been changed at the request of those involved. But I could have just as easily used your name because I'm convinced God wants this to be your story, too. He wants to include you in his great plan and do marvelous things that astound even you, all of which brings glory to the only name that really matters - His.

Throughout Scripture, God chose to work through weak, broken, and fallen men and women to accomplish remarkable things. Often, they were fearful and didn't want to obey: Gideon, Saul, Jonah. They messed up and were disobedient: Moses, David, Solomon. Many had huge failures in their past: Aaron, Peter, Paul. Many were of questionable character: Jacob, Rahab, Samson.

Some would say God used them in spite of their flaws. I'm convinced He used them *because* of their flaws. That way, there could be no question as to Who received the credit for the phenomenal things done through them.

We can all find reasons to believe God could never do miraculous things through us. It's not hard to list our disqualifications; I'm not smart enough, I'm not good enough, I've tried before and failed. I come from a bad background. I'm the wrong gender or the wrong race, born in the wrong place and at the wrong time in history. I'm not attractive. I don't have a charismatic personality. I have too many health problems. I never get any breaks. I've messed my life up too much. I've been messed up too much by others. I'm damaged goods. I don't have the proper education, experience, or credentials. I'm too old. I'm too young. Blah, blah, blah, blah.

But is it possible God ordained your upbringing, culture, financial situation, ethnicity, and even the tiniest aspects of your life for the specific purpose of doing amazing things through you to bring Him glory?

What if those natural disqualifiers are actually why God wants to use you? What if God is looking for people who know they don't have what it takes? What if He allowed those weaknesses and placed you in that imperfect family so He could do amazing things through you that He could then boast about throughout the ages?[3]

And here's some good news: God is never disappointed with you. Why? Because He never had any illusions about how wonderful you were in the first place. He remembers we're all just dust.[4]

1 Corinthians 1:26-30 gives us a checklist of qualifications God is looking for. Do you fit any of these: not wise, not influential, no special heritage, foolish, weak, humble, looked down on, counted as nothing? If any of these describe you, then you're qualified to get into God's toolbox and let Him use you for the purpose He designed and created you.

"Time is running out... The night is almost gone; the day of salvation will soon be here." Now, more than ever, we need to respond to the heart cry of Jesus - pray and ask the Lord to send more workers. After we pray we need to be part of the answer to the prayer.[5]

Your Piece Is Necessary

There's a place for each of us in completing the picture of the Great Commission. Perhaps you're to go. Perhaps you're to support others through giving, praying, encouraging, or advocating for them. Most missionaries I know do all of the above. Whatever piece you have in the Great Commission puzzle, no matter how insignificant it might appear to you, it's vital that you do your part and remain open to doing more: praying more, giving more, perhaps even going yourself. Your piece of the puzzle is needed.

A 10,000-piece puzzle is not complete if even a tiny piece is missing. And that missing piece, no matter how insignificant, stands out and mars the entire picture. Your piece is necessary. You are necessary. You are needed. Without your piece, the picture God is crafting is not complete.

My piece may seem small
In the plans of God's heart
But the picture's not finished
Till I do my part.

– RICK MALM

■　■　■

God is not looking for extraordinary characters
as His instruments, but He is looking for
humble instruments through whom He
can be honored throughout the ages.

– A.B. SIMPSON, FOUNDER OF THE CHRISTIAN
AND MISSIONARY ALLIANCE

CHAPTER 1

The Lord Is Able

■ ■ ■

"THE AVERAGE PERSON TODAY DOES not have the skills necessary to be a successful missionary."

That message, in huge letters, was on the front page of a missionary agency's website. My guess is they discouraged more folks than they convinced to apply.

Most of us already feel we don't have what it takes to be a missionary or, for that matter, to do anything significant for God. We imagine that God only uses super Christians. Folks who don't use bridges because they walk on water. Folks who don't use flashlights because the glow of their halo lights their way through the night.

We know that's not true, but still we feel there's something different about folks God uses to do amazing things. They're more talented. Their gifts and charisma are beyond the norm. They may not be "super Christians," but they sure aren't like you and me. They aren't just ordinary people.

I'm glad no one told me I didn't have what it took to be a successful missionary when, in the Summer of 1990, I felt God calling our young family to move to the war-torn country of Guatemala, Central America. There was already plenty to be concerned about. Would we be able to adjust to the culture? Could we learn the language? How would our three kids - ages twelve, ten, and five - deal with leaving home, family, and friends? How would we educate them? Would anyone support us? What were we doing moving to a country that had police death squads, random kidnappings and killings, Communist insurgents, rampant corruption, and the worst record of human rights violations of any Central American country?

The odds seemed so against us that I literally told my wife, "Jana, if we go and in a few months we realize we can't cut it, we'll just tuck our little tails between our legs and come home."

If, on the gasoline of all those insecurities, someone had tossed the match of, "By the way, you don't have what it takes," I'm pretty sure our missions career would have gone up in flames before it ever started. If "the average person" doesn't have what it takes, I sure didn't have a chance.

Off to a Flying Stop

My birth father was an alcoholic who became violent when he drank. I only have two memories of him and both involve hunting. I was no more than four years old, and I remember my grandparents frantically shoving me into the corner of a dilapidated tool shed, hiding me behind shovels, rakes, and yard tools. They told me to stay quiet because "your daddy is hunting for you." Through the rickety boards, I could see him and his rifle. He was drunk and hunting me to kill me. The second memory is of heavily armed police hunting my dad at night in a field across from our house. My dad hunting me and the police hunting my dad aren't the average father-son hunting stories most kids remember.

My mom met him while she was in high school. She was volunteering in a stateside Army hospital where he was a patient. He had broken his ankle jumping from a second-floor window when his girlfriend's husband arrived home earlier than expected. Rejecting all advice, Mom dropped out of high school to follow this guy who swept her off her feet.

A few years later, when she divorced, she had no skills, no car, and had to take whatever job she could find. That meant 40 hours a week dipping tennis shoes and boots in latex at a shoe factory located within walking distance of our government housing apartment in the ghetto of Rock Island, Illinois. The first bill she had to pay was to an elderly neighbor who looked after my two-year-old younger brother and me so mom could work.

Some time after the divorce, she met and married Douglas Malm, a wonderful man who became my dad and later adopted my brother and me. In fact, he said he married her because of the two boys that came with the deal. But he was obviously crazy about Mom because he gave up his dream hobby of racing sprint cars to begin providing for us.

Soon, we moved into what was a huge house for us at the time, but it grew smaller as our family grew to six kids. Looking back, I find it hard to believe all eight of us fit into a three-bedroom, one-bath house. That was our normal–but certainly below "average."

Learning the Value of Work

Six days a week, Dad left for work before sunrise, and I watched him drag home each evening covered in oil and dirt. He worked at E&J Metal Company: a fancy name for a junkyard. This place was an environmentalist's worst nightmare. It was acres and acres of rusting cars sitting on ground soaked in gasoline and oil, drained from the bellies of once-prized possessions. Hauled to their final resting place, these abandoned beauties now sat waiting to be cannibalized for a headlight, or a fender, or a bumper.

While we never went hungry, I often had holes in my shoes and pants— before it was cool to have holes in your pants. I thought nothing of it when I had to slip cardboard in the bottom of my shoes and put on rubber boots to keep the snow out.

From the age of eight, I delivered newspapers. My younger brother also got a paper route as soon as he was old enough. When Mom joined our newspaper delivery team with a huge "motor route," I went from riding a bike with a heavy bag draped over my shoulder to riding on the lowered tailgate of our faded green Chevy station wagon (that Dad had rescued from the junkyard).

In summer heat or winter blizzard, my younger brother, my mom, and I were out the door early enough to have all the papers delivered by 5:30 am. From the tailgate of that station wagon, my brother and I rolled, rubber banded, and tossed papers while my mom traced the familiar route, seven days a week.

In high school, I applied for other jobs, but never even got an interview. While most of my high school buddies were getting "real" jobs, I was embarrassed and tried to hide the fact that I was still a "paper*boy*," the job I'd earned as an eight-year-old (because I passed the test the route manager gave me: "If a customer owes you 75 cents and gives you a dollar, how much change do you give him?").

I could add and subtract, but algebra ate my lunch. A high school guidance counselor politely suggested I consider the "vocational track." I didn't even know what that meant, and my parents just trusted the school to make the right decision. "Vocational" sounded good to me because it meant no more math, chemistry, or physics.

Besides, college wasn't even a consideration for me because no one in my family had ever been to college. It was expensive and only for rich kids. That certainly left me out. As I neared the end of high school, I made plans to join the military after graduation.

My adoptive dad served in the Army during WWII, earned the Silver Star for heroism under fire as a medic, and was an active member of the American Legion. I was brought up on heavy doses of American patriotism and was regularly surrounded by World War II vets, so the military was a natural and honorable option.

CRAZY JESUS PEOPLE

Then, during my senior year of high school, I had a life-changing encounter with a group of "Jesus People" and then with Jesus himself. My family religiously attended Sunday School—not church—at the Moline Gospel Temple, a wonderful and very evangelistic Foursquare

Church. As a young child, I came to know the Lord, but I drifted away as a teen. I still saw myself as a Christian because that's what I did on Sunday. But it had no relevance to the way I lived my life Monday through Saturday.

But these crazy "Jesus People" talked about Jesus on Monday just like they did on Sunday. They lived for him 24/7, and I found that intriguing. Plus, they had some rocking good music and cute Jesus girls, which never hurts in leading teenage boys to the Lord (or anywhere else for that matter).

Their zeal was contagious and I got infected. I became a Jesus follower in 1971, halfway through my senior year of high school. But I had already early enlisted in the Navy, so it was still going to be "anchors away" for me.

ANCHORS AWAY

I loved the Navy. I loved being a Navy photographer–the job I was guaranteed before I enlisted. During my second year, I was transferred to the Naval Air Station in Corpus Christi, Texas, where I met my wife, Jana, at church. I was immediately smitten, and eventually convinced her to marry me. Like me, she had a passion for the Lord, but neither of us could have dreamed that our pursuit of Him would take us around the globe.

I was soon assigned to the Public Affairs Office for the admiral in charge of training all Navy and Marine pilots. It sounds like a prestigious position for an enlisted guy who joined right out of high school. In reality, it was a consequence that came about as a result of my not attending the weekend beer bashes hosted by my boss, a first-class petty officer, who regularly ridiculed me about my faith.

He transferred me to the admiral's staff to replace one of his drinking buddies who held that position. The staff position had a lot of weekend and after hour assignments that kept his buddy sober. By assigning me to that position, his buddy could now party with him, and the weekend assignments would interfere with my church attendance. He definitely saw it as a win-win.

I was one of four enlisted guys on the admiral's large staff. Suddenly I was surrounded by a whole world of educated, talented, highly-trained, and qualified people. Their uniforms had stars and bars, gold bling, and medals that reflected their accomplishments and military campaigns. These were America's finest, and then there was me. I was definitely a squid out of water.

A MOTIVATED FAILURE

My "below average" rating continued. Promotion for enlisted guys depended on your score on a test related to your job. The first time I took the test, I didn't even study. After all, I was a trained photographer. I did it every day. What was there to study? I knew this stuff.

Staring blankly at the test paper, I discovered there was a lot to study–and sadly, it included chemistry, physics, and a lot of other things that I squeaked out of studying in my high school vocational track.

The next year, I studied my little f-stop off and passed! But they had raised the requirement for promotion. I failed to advance again. On the third try, I missed promotion by 75/100th of a point! Other guys I worked with were putting on stripes, but I was stuck–Mr. Below Average.

The ultimate insult came in 1976, when I got a letter from the personnel office in Washington, D.C. The Vietnam War was over, and the Navy was downsizing. I had failed to be promoted. The wording was very military but basically, the Navy was firing me! Based on my failure to be promoted they determined I was "unmotivated."

But I was highly motivated. I just didn't have what it took. Just call me, "Petty Officer Below Average." And yet, God chose to do some extraordinary things with my very ordinary life.

THE TYPE OF PERSON GOD USES

Once upon a time, we all dreamed of doing extraordinary things. As children, we imagined ourselves hitting the winning home run, being chosen as the lead singer or dancer, being crowned #1, or winning the gold medal. Not one of us dreamed of being a failure.

That yearning within us to do something exceptional is part of the divine spark God places in each of us. We were designed by Him to do great things that reflect honor back to Him.[6]

Because of that, we should want to make our lives count, by doing great things to glorify God. William Carey, the father of modern missions, put it this way: "Expect great things *from* God. Attempt great things *for* God."

But life has a way of slapping us down. Our dreams get trampled and crushed until they fit into the tiny box of our own abilities. We begin to believe we can't do anything great because we don't have the pedigrees, the charisma, the talents, the confidence, or the strengths that others have.

My box was certainly small and limited. I had a messed up background. I knew the flaws of my heart. Like sparrows darting from tree to tree, I knew every evil thought that seemed to flash uncontrollably through my brain. I knew how calloused, insensitive, judgmental, and proud I could be. I was certainly not like the sweet, got-it-all-together Christian people I found myself surrounded by at church.

In many ways, my Christianity felt like my assignment on the admiral's staff. I was a barely-high-school-grad enlisted kid surrounded by America's finest officers: highly trained, highly skilled jet pilots and leaders, men of action and experience. At church, I felt the same way. There were so many gifted and talented people that God would certainly use to do amazing things—and then there was me, Mr. Less Than Average.

Some of us have messed up our lives pretty badly. Some of us have been messed up by others. Would God really choose ordinary people like you and me when there are so many skilled, talented, trained and gifted people He could choose instead?

Yes!

In Jesus' day, the most talented, educated, and gifted Bible scholars, teachers, seminarians, and religious people in the world were in Jerusalem. It was full of keepers of the law, people with perfect pedigrees and spotless backgrounds.

Surely Jesus should have gone to the temple school and conducted interviews to find His disciples. He could have found the most brilliant, talented communicators and scholars of His day. They were right there, gathered in Jerusalem, willing and wanting to serve God.

He was picking men for the most challenging and crucial mission ever committed to man. There was no plan B. They absolutely had to succeed.

We're so familiar with the story that it loses its shock value, but for literally the most important task of all time, God didn't choose a single Bible scholar. He didn't choose a single theologian. He didn't choose a single qualified person.

He chose "ignorant and unlearned fishermen."[7] He chose a low-level government employee. He chose a political radical. He chose the "foolish things to shame the wise."[8] He chose Mr. Below Average.

This has always been God's method. Gideon was fear-drenched and hiding from the enemy when God chose him to be His mighty man of valor. God bypassed every battle-hardened soldier in the Israeli army and chose young David to confront Goliath. Many of the men who rallied around David had sketchy backgrounds, but they became his mighty men who accomplished extraordinary feats.[9]

God did choose an outstanding man to be Israel's first king. The Bible says there was not a better man in all Israel than Saul.[10] But Saul failed miserably. Then God chose David, who was such an unlikely pick that even David's own father overlooked him. God prefers a good-hearted David to a good-looking Saul.

That's why I totally reject the idea that the "average person" is unqualified and inadequate. I firmly believe God uses ordinary people to accomplish extraordinary work.

THE ONLY LIMITATION IS GOD'S ABILITY

Romans 14:4 asks, "Who are you to judge someone else's servant?"[11] Who am I to determine what God can or cannot do through this man or that woman?

There's no way personality profiles, psychological tests, interviews or other screening techniques can predict what God is going to do through His servant. When the Lord gets involved He becomes this giant X factor. This man, this woman, has these limitations and can only go this far. But when God steps in the results can be beyond our imagination.

When a man or woman is walking in obedience, the limits are no longer the tiny box of his or her abilities. The only limitation is God's ability. God delights to take the least and the last and make them the first and the best. In fact, sometimes, our abilities become a hindrance for the Divine One to overcome. "He must become greater. I must become less."[12]

"Who are you to judge someone else's servant?"[13] The passage goes on to state, "They will stand or fall before their own master. And they will stand, for the Lord is able to make them stand."[14]

Did you catch the last part of that verse? They *will* stand. They won't stand because of their personal pedigree, talent, or training. They *will* stand; they will succeed, because "the Lord is able."

You and I can do amazing things because He is able. You can see that incredible dream God put in your heart become a reality because He is able.

This isn't about you. This isn't about me. This isn't about what we want to do. This is about God making His name great. This is about what He wants to do. But He wants to make His name great by using you and me.

When I judge someone as unable, I'm really saying God's not able. When I judge myself as unable, I declare the same lie. I'm saying God's not able. But God wants to prove us wrong. He wants to prove that He's able to accomplish amazing things, even through you and me.

The Lord loves to take a below average, incapable, unqualified person and do remarkable things through him ... because it demonstrates that He is able.

WHERE DO YOU START TO MAKE THAT GOD-DREAM A REALITY?

My story, along with the stories of many others, has convinced me that anyone can be a missionary. In fact, I'm convinced you can do anything God puts in your heart. But you need to start right where you are.

Take the first step you can take to make that God-dream come true. You don't have to know all the steps on the path. You just need to know the next step. And take it.

What can you do today to make your marriage great? What can you do today to be a better employee, to be a better boss, to be a better parent, to be a better friend? What can you do today to write that book, start that business, to fulfill the dream God deposited in your heart?

Faith requires action. Do what you can, and watch God do what only He can do. This is all about Him bringing honor to Himself by accomplishing extraordinary things through very ordinary people.

If you had told me God was going to use me to start a mission agency that would send thousands of ordinary people around the world, I wouldn't have believed it. In fact, I still have moments when I don't believe it.

This book is about how God did extraordinary things through an ordinary guy. My goal is to show you that you can do anything God puts in your heart – no matter how unqualified you are – because your disqualification is the first qualification God looks for.

Now that I've been at this mission and ministry thing for over 40 years, I think the statement on that missions website has a kernel of truth in it. If you are an average person, you don't have what it takes - and that's exactly why God wants to use you.

Father, I feel so inadequate.
And I'm glad I do.
Cause Lord, if I were adequate,
I'd have no need of You.

- UNKNOWN

■　■　■

Missionaries are very human folks ...simply
a bunch of nobodies trying to exalt
Somebody.

- JIM ELLIOT, MISSIONARY MARTYR TO ECUADOR

CHAPTER 2

I Didn't Think You Had A Chance

■ ■ ■

IN 1976, AS I WAS being discharged from the Navy, my pastor invited me to join the staff of the church my wife and I attended in Corpus Christi, Texas. He encouraged me to use my military benefits and go to college while helping the church with their printing needs, operating the sound system, and doing whatever I could to serve. In exchange, they would pay me $100 a week.

God's certainly not opposed to training and education, and there's no virtue in ignorance. Repeatedly the Bible tells us to "get wisdom," to study to show ourselves approved. Ecclesiastes compares education to sharpening an axe. It's easier to cut down a tree with a sharp axe than with a dull one.[15]

It's true, God used "unschooled, ordinary" fishermen,[16] but the two men who wrote the majority of the New Testament—Paul and Luke—were both highly educated. There's no shame in being "unschooled," but we shouldn't take pride in staying that way, either.

Unschooled Peter tells us we shouldn't stay ignorant - "make every effort to add to your faith goodness; and to goodness, knowledge."[17]

While highly educated Paul had to lay aside "lofty words and impressive wisdom." He had to reduce his message to nothing but "Jesus Christ and him crucified."[18]

The Key To Being Used By God

We shouldn't think God can't use us because we lack education, but we should also take advantage of every opportunity to learn and "sharpen the axe." The key here is humility. If we're proud of our education or proud of our ignorance, God Himself will stand against our efforts. He resists the proud.[19]

For the next four years, I worked about thirty-five hours a week at the church, went to college full time, and graduated with a BA in Business. Upon my graduation, the elders responsible for the church's Christian school asked to meet with me.

"We have an unchristian school in a Christian school–especially the high school," they told me. "We want you to be the school Principal and change that."

I was only 25 years old. My own children were preschoolers. My new degree was in business. I had no idea how to run a school, let alone help a failing one recover. I knew I was completely unqualified, way over my head. The odds were totally against me being able to pull this off.

There was only one reasonable answer.

"Let's do it!"

This was one of my first experiences of seeing God use the unqualified–me. I knew that if I didn't completely lean on Him, I was going to fail miserably. Within four years, the school was transformed. But it was clearly the work of the Lord through an amazing staff, and of the Holy Spirit in the lives of the students.

I decided if I was going to be a school principal, I should learn something about it. So, I started back to school using the remainder of my GI Bill to earn a Master in Educational Administration.

While working toward that degree, the pastor who invited me to join the church staff left Corpus Christi to start a missionary training center in the Hill Country of Texas. Later, he asked me to join him in this risky venture. I was to help plant and pastor a church connected with the soon-to-appear missionary training center.

I was close to finishing my degree in Education. I was just beginning to feel competent leading the school, and now I was being invited to launch into something else I wasn't qualified for.

Shocking News from my Pastor

What did I know about missions? Not much. What did I know about planting a church? Even less. But my wife, Jana, and I both felt it was God calling us to step out and take the risk. It meant a 50% cut in salary, with the odds hugely stacked against us. But in February of 1986, we moved our three kids from the comfort and security of the established church that my wife had been part of all her life, to this risky new venture seven miles outside of Kerrville, Texas.

During this time, I worked very closely with the pastor who first invited me into ministry, and he told me something that was a little shocking. I had served by his side almost twelve years when he said, "The only reason I hired you out of the Navy was that I clearly heard God tell me to. I thought you were the most unlikely candidate for ministry I'd ever met. I didn't think you had a chance to make it."

Ouch! I'm glad he didn't tell me that 12 years earlier. But, I have to admit, he was right. I was an unlikely candidate for ministry and, by all natural measures, I didn't have a chance to succeed. The odds were radically stacked against me.

I think those are the odds God loves most—impossible ones. Why else would He tell Gideon to send most of his army home? Why else would He send a fugitive from the law back to Egypt armed with only a stick to confront the most powerful leader on the face of the Earth? Why else would He surround the tiny nation of Israel with huge and powerful enemies? Why else would He call you to do the impossible dream that He has put in your heart?

I'm convinced it's because God loves impossible odds.

Against all odds, this less than average, very ordinary guy, who couldn't get promoted in the Navy, made it through college–with honors. This guy, who was channeled into the vocational track in high school, prepared scores of other high schoolers to excel in college. This guy, with no seminary or Bible school training, established a healthy church that saw many lives impacted by the gospel.

God seems to get a big kick out of using ordinary, unqualified people. He seems zealously committed to making sure the glory remains His. But God wasn't finished showing His ability through my inability.

After pastoring for four years, Jana and I both began to sense God calling us into something new. We had no idea what it would be. If it followed the pattern of the past, He would launch us, once again, into an arena where we were totally over our heads. And that's just what He did.

How To Proceed When You Aren't Sure

We received a call from Steve, the founder of a mission agency that sent short-term teams to Central America. Steve's brother, David, was a good friend we had visited in Guatemala. Steve asked if we would move our family to Guatemala to head up their team of missionaries there. Specifically, he wanted me to start a training program for new missionaries who wanted to join his organization, Missionary Ventures.

It was actually quite laughable. I had never been a missionary. I had never lived outside the United States. The missionary training center we were trying to start in Texas was a total failure. Despite hundreds of thousands of dollars and four years of prayer, sweat, and tears, we never managed to send a single missionary. I didn't have a large network of contacts, and this new position required us to raise our own support. He wanted me to train missionaries? Are you kidding?

We prayed. In my heart I felt it was an invitation from the Lord, but we didn't hear any voices or receive any Earth-shattering confirmations. Jana was less sure than me, but was willing to follow, trusting that God would guide us.

I have to admit, I envy folks who hear so clearly from the Lord that they have no doubt about God's calling. It's never been that way for me. My following the Lord has always been more like "onward through the fog."

I've never been 100% certain–at least not until after I make the commitment and step out of the boat. When I'm about 70% sure I'm hearing from the Lord, I start moving forward, taking baby steps and asking Him to stop me if I'm headed the wrong direction. He's always been faithful to do so.

We decided we'd take this missions invitation one baby step at a time. If it wasn't the Lord, He could close the door at any time (and we fully expected Him to, because there were many good reasons we had no business going into the mission field).

Due to the financial struggles, pressures of a new church, and our own immaturity, our marriage was at an all-time low. Jana was enduring physical pain that the doctor, after extensive and expensive testing, concluded was "stress." Our kids didn't want to go–the oldest was adamant and vocal in his opposition. In nearly every category, we were a mess of stress–certainly not impressive candidates for missions, but we sensed God saying, "Go."

Baby step #1 - Get counsel. I went to an older pastor who had counseled Jana and me, and was a dear friend to both of us. "Sam, you know we've been struggling in our marriage. You know the pressure we've been under trying to establish this church and the missionary training center. You know the stress-related physical problems Jana's been battling, and you know we have three young kids. But I feel God is calling us to move to Guatemala and serve with Missionary Ventures."

He pointed out the obvious. "You know moving to Central America as missionaries is not a way to lessen stress."

"I know." I responded. "But what do you do when you feel like it's what God is saying you should do?"

His answer: "You obey."

"That's what I thought," I said, "I just needed to hear it from someone older and wiser."

We would obey what we sensed the Lord saying and take the next baby step. But surely this one would trip us up and put an end to this crazy missionary venture.

Baby step #2 - Meet the Board. We went to interview with the board of Missionary Ventures. We didn't want any surprises, so we decided we would let them know up front that we were struggling in our marriage, that we didn't know anything about training missionaries, and that we weren't sure we could raise enough support to go. Surely they would decide we weren't the folks for this job, and that would be the end of it.

The personnel committee of the board consisted of a couple of doctors and an insurance agent. Jana and I told them we were excited about the opportunity and that we wanted to go, but we also told them about our doubts, fears, and struggles. We let them know all the reasons it was a crazy idea and why we were totally unqualified to do it. They asked a lot of insightful questions and listened to our story.

Though they listened, they obviously either didn't hear a word we said, or they believed God was going to bring glory to His name by using this ordinary, unqualified, struggling couple. They unanimously asked us to be the newest missionaries with Missionary Ventures.

Big step #1 – Overcome barriers. We returned home astounded that God had kept the door open. But there were still many barriers. We had to sell a home at a time when Texas was experiencing a financial crisis. Several homes in our neighborhood sat empty and could be acquired from the bank by simply starting to make the monthly payment on the mortgage.

Big step #2 – Raise support. We had to raise our own support to provide for a family of five. We had to raise additional funds to cover moving and costs to establish a home in Guatemala. We would also have expenses related to language school. The church we'd been pastoring was struggling financially, so we knew they couldn't help. Our congregation had several unemployed families, and it labored under a huge burden of debt and overhead expenses because of the vision for a missionary training center.

We didn't have a large network of people to appeal to, and we had no rich uncle waiting in the wings to help. God was going to have to work overtime if this was going to happen.

The Thing That Scares The Bravest of Missionaries

So many folks come to Commission To Every Nation (CTEN) in the exact situation as Jana and I – step-by-step, following the Lord and trusting Him to guide and provide day by day. They have an opportunity open to them, and they want to go, but they wonder if they can conquer all the obstacles. The scariest one is usually raising the funds to go.

Most of us don't mind asking people to pray for us. But, to actually ask them to give money? Well, that's humbling and hard.

Eating bugs, sleeping on bamboo mats, sweltering heat, weird diseases and all the typical missionary trials people think about can be challenging. But most missionaries do OK with those hardships. "After all," we reason, "If we survive this thing, it's going to make an awesome story for our next newsletter! Be sure and take pictures, honey." But raising support? I think I'd rather eat termite larvae and monkey meat.

When I first started raising support to go to Guatemala, I probably would have never had the courage to share our needs with anyone, but Proverbs 16:26 was looming on the horizon. It says (and I'm paraphrasing), "Hunger is a good thing because it motivates the worker to get to work." If I didn't "get to work" asking folks to join our support team, I was going to quickly be motivated by three hungry kids and a wife.

I had already stepped out of the boat. I had resigned from my job as pastor. The church leadership promised 6 months of salary while I raised support. But after recalculating they revised it to only 6 weeks. I was grateful for any help, but it meant I didn't have much time. I had to make that first "will-you-help-us" call.

I decided to call a pastor friend who I was sure would say, "Yes." I needed a small victory to get started. I was too timid to ask him to personally support us or even ask him to put us in the church's missions budget. I was just going to see if I could come and share our vision for about five minutes with some of the folks in his congregation, hoping maybe some would want to get on board with us.

My request was met with an explanation that they were in a building program and funds were tight.

"Oh, I understand. I'm not asking you to put us in the church budget. I'd just like to come and briefly share what God has called us to do and see if anyone might be interested in being part of it with us."

Another excuse.

Again, I tried to make it clear. I wasn't asking for anything but an opportunity to share our vision. Surely he was just misunderstanding what I was asking.

After the third excuse, it dawned on me, "He's saying, 'No! Absolutely not.'"

I hung up the phone, devastated. This was my ace-in-the-hole, and it was a total miss. My missions career was over before it even began. If this friend and fellow pastor wouldn't even give me five minutes to share with his small congregation, who was going to actually believe in us enough to send real money?

Trapped At the Red Sea? Remember Who Led You There

Like our situation, many new CTENers come from tiny churches that are behind them spiritually but are not able to help financially. Most don't have a huge network of contacts to appeal to for help. All feel awkward asking for help and many have been told directly by their families that they should stop this missions nonsense and "get a real job."

They don't know who to ask. They don't know how to ask. They don't want to ask. But that's what they have to do. No country wants them coming and taking jobs from national workers to fund themselves. Plus, if they did go and get a "real job," most of their time would be spent making a living and just doing all the extra things it takes to live in another country. There would be little time to devote to their ministry.

Here again, we see that God has stacked the deck against Himself and His people. He has sent Gideon's army home. He has pitted a young shepherd boy against a skilled giant of a warrior. He has trapped his people between the Red Sea and Pharaoh's angry army.

When you face that sort of impossibility–and if you haven't already, you will–it's important to realize this is God's modus operandi: just the way He likes to do things. Sometimes it will look like the wall you face is due to your own bad planning. That's what Israel said to Moses, "Why did you bring us out here?" But it was God, not Moses, Who led them into a hopeless situation trapped on the shores of the Red Sea.

Sometimes it will look like a stroke of bad luck, as in Job's case when everything in his life fell apart all at the same time. Sometimes the obstacles will be so overwhelming and so final that it will appear your dream is beyond hope and totally dead–as dead as the hope the disciples had that their murdered leader would be the promised Messiah.

But if you've been following God into this venture–even if only 70% sure it's Him–you can be confident that this impossibility is God saying, "I've got this one. Stand back and watch." He parted the sea for Moses. He restored more back to Job than he had lost. He raised Jesus Christ from the dead. And the same power that delivered God's people in the Old and New Testament is at work fulfilling His dream and desire in you.

Where do you begin to raise enough support to move to Central America and sustain a family of five? Where do you begin to fulfill an impossible dream? You start by doing what you can do and then trust God to do what only He can do.

We sent a personalized letter to everyone we could think of telling them about this new direction and asking them to partner with us financially.

It was awkward. It was hard to ask. What would people think? Would it damage some friendships when we talked with them about money? We sent the letters and waited. And waited. No response at all.

It was too late to back out now. We had already resigned from the church. We had managed to miraculously sell our home – in 10 days, for a fair price and to a cash buyer who also wanted to buy our furniture! But no support was coming in. We were standing on the shores of the Red Sea. There was no turning back. We were committed–and sometimes thinking we should have been committed for being crazy.

A month later, we sent a second letter. And again all we knew to do was wait. I'll never forget the day we got a response from an older couple we knew years before. They wrote to say they would send us $10 a month. That was the sweetest $10 imaginable. Someone actually believed in us. Maybe, just maybe, God was again going to show Himself able–able to make His servants stand.

ANYBODY CAN BE A MISSIONARY

One by one, God carried us over each of the hurdles. Our first financial partner was joined by a few others. The miraculous way our home sold was a great assurance to Jana that God was in this thing. We took every opportunity we could find to share what we were doing—Bible studies, a nursing home chapel, individuals we'd run into in the grocery store or on the street. We even got a couple of opportunities to speak at churches and meet some new people.

It was after speaking at one of these churches that something happened to remind me that this was not about us. This was about a great

God who had a mission He wanted to accomplish. And He was using this unqualified, very ordinary couple to do it so it would be clear Who deserved the credit.

I spoke at a small Spanish-speaking congregation. "How ironic," I thought. "I'm asking all these Spanish speaking people to support a gringo to go learn Spanish and minister to Spanish speakers."

I poured my heart out, and after the message, the pastor (who I had only met a couple of times) came to the platform to close the service. It was obvious he was deeply moved. Was it my message? Was it a burden he felt for missions? What had shaken him to his core?

Slowly and deliberately he explained. "As a boy, I heard Jim Elliot speak. Since that day, I've had a reverence for missionaries. I thought they were super Christians, beyond the normal. Today, as I heard Brother Malm speak, I realized: anybody can be a missionary."

Call me crazy, but I took that as a compliment. In fact, probably one of the highest compliments I've ever received.

Pastor Ortiz was absolutely right. God doesn't look for super men or super women. He seeks ordinary ones that He can do the extraordinary through. He doesn't require us to be courageous and great visionaries—Gideon and Moses weren't. He doesn't even require us to be totally obedient–David and Samson weren't. He simply looks for ones who will respond to His invitation by saying, "Here I am. Send me." (Which even Moses, Jonah, and Gideon only did reluctantly.)

Yes, anybody can be a missionary, but I had no idea how much that statement would be walked out in my life. Four years later, I would be starting an agency with the goal of making it simple for anybody to respond to that call of God: "Whom shall I send and who will go for us?"

Four years later I would be "Helping Ordinary People Partner With God To Accomplish The Extraordinary."

Hardship often prepares an ordinary
person for an extraordinary destiny.

- C.S. LEWIS, BRITISH NOVELIST, POET
AND CHRISTIAN APOLOGIST

■　■　■

God uses men who are weak and
feeble enough to lean on Him.

- HUDSON TAYLOR, MISSIONARY TO CHINA AND
FOUNDER OF THE CHINA INLAND MISSION

CHAPTER 3

Already Tried That And Totally Failed

■ ■ ■

We loved Guatemala!

Even our children, who were initially opposed to going, fell in love with their new Latin American home.

I loved the language, the culture, the food, the people, our co-workers, and the national ministers we served with. I loved leading teams and everything else we were doing with Missionary Ventures. Even the random police checkpoints and regular attempts to extort a bribe were part of the exotic charm for me.

We enjoyed the cool climate of our home at seven thousand feet and the two spectacular volcanoes that greeted us each morning. Pacaya often showed off by spewing lava thousands of feet into the air. The weather was "boringly perfect" every day. We were living in paradise!

Yes, there were challenges. Occasionally, the Communist-backed guerrillas blew up an electrical tower somewhere in the country. Often, that plunged the capital city below us–Guatemala City—into darkness. But our little corner of heaven was even protected from that inconvenience.

We lived in the shadow of three crucial military communication towers. They were well guarded and keeping them operational was a strategic priority, which also benefited us.

I drove from our home in San Lucas, Sacatapequez, to Antigua each morning to study Spanish–fulfilling a life-long dream. My "classroom" was the flat roof of the Centro Linguistico Maya where I sat across from my private tutor at a 3-foot-by-2-foot handmade table. I often found it hard to focus on my studies because I was overwhelmed by the sheer beauty surrounding me–and my brain quickly overdosed on verb endings and conjugations.

It was like living on the pages of National Geographic–cobblestone streets, four hundred year old archaeological ruins from three historic earthquakes, and colorful plastered walls that often revealed ancient adobe bricks where sections of the plaster had fallen away. The cascading bougainvilleas and three volcanoes graced the city with color and majesty. The warm days and cool breeze made it all almost too much to take in. No wonder they call it, "The Land of Eternal Springtime."

We put the kids in a Guatemalan school–not so good. Then we homeschooled with help from Terri Jacobs. I was Terri's principal when she was in junior high and even then she was interested in missions. She went on to get her teaching certificate and the Lord miraculously reconnected us just when we needed a teacher. What a double blessing–she got to be a missionary, and we got a teacher!

She taught the two older ones–—Joel and Charis—while Jana worked with Jonathan. It was a great experience, and it meant the kids could go with us when we led teams into villages and the beautiful Guatemalan countryside.

When Terri met and married a missionary doing agricultural work, we put the kids in the Christian Academy of Guatemala–a school started by missionaries to educate missionary kids (MKs). We didn't know it at the time, but both the agricultural missionary who stole our teacher's heart and the Christian Academy of Guatemala would play an important part in what God would do in us in just a few years. But at the time, we were totally enjoying serving with a great team and blessing the people of the land we joyously called home.

Of course there were struggles and frustrations. We regularly had to deal with government bureaucracy. I'm convinced the anti-Christ runs immigration offices around the world. There was police corruption--which, once you learn the system, can actually work to your benefit. Some of the areas where we worked were unsafe places to travel at night–sometimes even during the day–due to the Communist–backed insurgents who set up roadblocks and collected a "war tax." They could be very persuasive in convincing you to pay your fair share (aka, all you had with you at the time).

Then there were random protests, riots, shootings, and robberies. In six years we were robbed, swindled, or broken into six times. When we compared notes with other missionaries, we discovered we were right on track–the average missionary experienced one crime a year.

But there was a grace that carried us through even these "light and momentary troubles." [20] I settled in, hoping and expecting to be in Guatemala the rest of my life. But four short years later, God started messing with my little paradise.

I Want You To Bless The Nations

A guest speaker from the states came to encourage the missionaries. His message reminded us of God's promise to bless all families on earth through Abraham's seed. Jesus——the seed—came and made salvation available to those who believe; but until people hear they cannot believe. [21] It was encouraging to be reminded that we, as missionaries, work with God to make sure "all families on earth" hear so they can be blessed. That means missionaries are partnering with God to fulfill a four-thousand-year-old promise He made to a friend—Abraham.

Great message, especially inspiring for missionaries, but then it got personal. Over the next few months, whenever I prayed, my mind would become muddled with the thought, "I want you to bless the nations." God seemed to be personalizing this promise to Abraham. He seemed to be repeating it to me as a command, "Bless the nations."

At first it was like a distracting gnat buzzing in my brain. But as months passed, it grew in volume and became more and more irritating. It felt like a heavy burden I was carrying. I couldn't focus on reading. I couldn't focus on praying. I thought it was the voice of the Holy Spirit, but it couldn't be.

Bless the nations? Me?

If this was God calling, He had surely dialed a wrong number. I had a track record to prove I was not the guy to do this.

Been There, Done That, Failed Miserably

Remember the little church we planted in Kerrville, Texas, before we came to Guatemala? Did I mention that the church was called "Trinity **World Outreach?**"

Two years after we left, it closed its doors. There was no missionary training center. There was no church. There was no "world outreach." In the natural, it looked like a total failure.

Prior to my arriving at Trinity World Outreach, the founder, armed with a vision for training missionaries, chose that lofty name, hired a full-time director for the soon-to-appear Doulos Missionary Training Center, and secured a loan to purchase eighteen acres of land outside of town (land surrounded by nothing but ranches, ticks and mesquite trees).

Those eighteen acres and a staff salary meant the tiny congregation–of perhaps twenty faith-filled people–was in debt to the bank for $250,000.00 and had a monthly budget in excess of $5,000. Now there was the added expense of a salary for their new pastor—me.

On top of the impossible financial situation, we were a start-up church located so far outside of town that it was a long-distance call to reach our offices. If location, location, location is important then our situation was bad, bad, and really bad. In every way, this venture was a jumbo jet blasting toward earth for an inevitable, explosive crash landing.

For four years, we fought leaky roofs, duct-taped antiquated air conditioners, cleaned up after broken plumbing, and endured trials with water wells, pumps, and septic systems. We were plagued with scorpions and demon fire ants that liked to accumulate in such mass around the electrical breaker boxes that they eventually shorted out the box, frying thousands of ants and throwing the entire complex into darkness.

On top of that, there were interpersonal challenges with the congregation and leadership and those bothersome creditors who liked to get paid now and then. No wonder my marriage and family were struggling.

But, for four years we also saw eternal destinies changed, people coming to know Jesus and growing in their walk with God. We endured tough times with some wonderful praying people. I learned what it means to pastor, to preach and teach, to serve people in times of great rejoicing and in the deepest of unexplainable sorrows.

We saw God deliver people from demonic oppression and generational bondages. We even saw God miraculously meet the budget every month. With a few late fees and much grace from our creditors, we were able to keep the lights on the entire time.

Were we reaching the world? Not hardly. We barely reached the neighbors and the closest town. Through lots of effort, the tiny congregation of about twenty skyrocketed to about sixty on a good Sunday–but there weren't many good Sundays. We always had more chickens, goats, rabbits, and cats–lots of feral cats—than we had people on our sprawling eighteen-acre campus.

As the pastor, I have to admit I was always a little embarrassed about the name "World Outreach." Especially when I met other pastors in town who were leading churches with less ostentatious names but who actually had a world outreach as well as doing amazing things to impact our area.

The missionary training center? Oh, we did have a student or two who dropped in for a few months–primarily because it was free. One hardy young man actually hung around for the two year "program" (I use that word loosely). Undoubtedly the best thing he got out of his experience was a wife. Did we actually send any missionaries? Strangely enough, after four years, we did send one family—mine.

The Path to the Promised Land

Like us, if you're going to be used by God, you're going to face some fire. Finding yourself in a hot, dry wilderness doesn't mean God has abandoned you. The road to the promised land runs right through that wilderness. Learning to cling to Him in the isolation and desolation is part of God's preparation process. No one is greatly used by God who has not been greatly tested.

The testing is designed to break us so He can reshape us. As John Wimber, founder of the Vineyard Churches, often said, "I don't trust any leader that doesn't walk with a limp"–an obvious reference to Jacob's time of testing while wrestling with the Lord.[22] Like a man who strikes the ice of a frozen river to test its strength before walking on it, God tests those He's going to use. And, like a good teacher who keeps quiet while students are testing, God may seem far away when you feel you need Him the most.

But unlike tests you took in school, all God's tests are open Book. In fact, you're encouraged to look in the Book for answers. The author of the textbook is never far away if you need help understanding it. And if you fail, it doesn't go on your permanent record. You just get to take the test again and again–as many times as necessary until you pass. And the most encouraging news is that a test is an indication that, once you pass, you're ready to be promoted to greater things.

Trinity World Outreach was a missionary testing center for my family and me. It had moments of soaring victories but also deep, dark valleys. During one "dark night of the soul"[23] I discovered a principle that helped me endure–the deeper the pit, the higher the peak.

The Deeper the Pit, The Higher the Peak

As I dredged Scripture looking for encouragement, I saw that those who successfully endured the hardest tests were also used for the greatest purposes by the Lord. Moses spent 40 years in hiding. Joseph went from favorite son to a pit, to slavery, and then to prison. Paul knew hunger and thirst, persecution, beatings, shipwrecks, stoning, and imprisonment. All these extremely deep pits led to extremely high mountaintop experiences of being used by God.

Others in Scripture endured less pain, less loss, and less grief, but they were typically also used to a lesser degree by the Father. The pit is proportional to the peak. And, of course, Jesus is the ultimate example of being plunged into the deepest pit of death, only to be resurrected to the highest peak–King of kings and Lord of lords, to Whom every knee shall bow.

That encouraged me to endure the pit, even to embrace its depth. You can be sure God doesn't bring you down to abandon you. He will also bring you out. And you can be certain there will be a glorious view waiting for you on the other side of the pit.

"You have allowed me to suffer much hardship, but you will restore me to life again and lift me up from the depths of the earth."[24]

Pits Produce Power

Often, like Joseph, who was thrown in a pit by his own brothers, it's other Christians who toss you into the pit. If you've been in the church for a while, especially in a position of leadership, you've likely been hurt by other believers. God's sheep have fangs and, sadly, many feel justified to use them to bite and devour others in the family. After a particularly difficult situation in my own ministry life, I complained to God, "I'd be a terrible father if I allowed my kids to treat one another the way You allow Your kids to. You let insecure leaders use and abuse people. You let hurting people hurt people. We cut, slash, and devour one another. Yet You stand idly by and do nothing to stop it. How can You let all that happen?"

Over the next few months, I began to understand that the fruit of the spirit only grows in bad soil. If I'm never mistreated, abused, or persecuted, how can I learn to bless, forgive, and pray for those that abuse me? Unless I face something, or someone, that severely tries my patience, how can I learn to be patient? It's only in the valley of the shadow of death that I learn to fear no evil. Pits, attacks, and pain are an opportunity to grow more into the image of our Lord.

Anyone can love the lovable. But the bad soil in the bottom of the pit allows us to develop love for those we would naturally despise. Like the Holy Spirit drove Jesus into the wilderness, He will lead us to the pit so we might be tested. Jesus went into the wilderness filled with the Holy Spirit but He came out in the power of the Spirit.[25] The pit produces power.

As believers (and as human beings) we see pain, suffering, and sorrow as something to avoid at all costs. But God says they are the path to reigning with Christ, the necessary path to glorification, something to rejoice over.[26] A.W. Tozer nailed it when he said, "It is doubtful whether God can bless a man greatly until He has hurt him deeply." Even God's own Son couldn't accomplish His mission without pain and the pit.

But this idea of persecution and suffering becomes very real when we discuss it in a missionary context. In day-to-day church-speak, persecution means the guys at school laughed at me, or I didn't get the raise because I'm too religious. But in the missions context, persecution and suffering can take on life-and-death status.

How to Stay Safe

"Is it safe to go there?" is a question that's often asked when someone announces a call to a foreign mission field. The standard answers are "Is there any place that's truly safe?" and "The safest place to be is in the center of God's will." From an eternal perspective those are both absolutely true. But if you look at the lives of James and Peter, Paul and Polycarp, thousands of saints throughout church history, Jim Elliot and his four companions in Ecuador, and thousands martyred by opponents of the cross up to this day, you find that "the safest place to be" may lead to suffering and death.

If our goal is safety, then we need to stop sending missionaries. But if our goal is to glorify God with our lives, then we are left with only one option—obedience. As Mark Batterson, pastor of National Community Church in Washington, D.C. and author of "Chase the Lion" says, "There comes a moment when you have to quit living as if the purpose of life is to arrive safely at death. The will of God is not an insurance plan. The will of God is a dangerous plan. The will of God might get you killed."

Everyone who is passionate about following God, including Jesus himself, gets acquainted with Sorrow.[27] So don't be surprised, as if something strange were happening, if you encounter sorrow, pain, loss, or discouragement when you set out to seriously follow the Lord. Especially if you're following Him into an arena that confronts the forces of darkness head on.

When you find yourself in the pit, you can be sure God didn't bring you there to leave you. Nor is this time wasted. Daniel spent time in a pit. Joseph spent time in a pit. Jeremiah spent time in a pit. Paul spent time in the pit of a Roman prison. And our own Lord spent time buried in the pit of the Earth. Only then could He experience resurrection power.

God delivered Daniel, Joseph, Jeremiah and Jesus. Paul's pit allowed him time to write the letters that comprise much of our New Testament. Pits serve God's purpose. Pits prepare God's people. Pits are part of His perfecting plan.

So, "Dear brothers and sisters, when troubles come your way, consider it an opportunity for great joy. For you know that when your faith is tested, your endurance has a chance to grow. So let it grow, for when your endurance is fully developed, you will be perfect and complete, needing nothing."[28]

You will be perfect and complete, needing nothing. That's why you're facing the trial, the obstacles, the pain, and the persecution. That's the reason for the pit. God is not against you. He is at work perfecting you. So rejoice.

I'm Going to Give You a Team

We were loving Guatemala. When we left the struggling church plant, we felt like we had been delivered from a pit and now, we were quite literally walking on the mountaintops of Central America. I had no plans of ever doing anything else.

But four years after we left that failed church plant and world outreach ministry, God seemed to be saying, "I want you to bless the nations." Do you see the irony in that? For obvious reasons, I was slightly bothered by what appeared to be God toying with me.

"God, we already tried the bless-the-nations-thing. Remember Trinity **World Outreach**? It flopped. Can't you leave me alone? Let me just bless Guatemala."

But when I tried to pray or read the Bible, the noise in my head wouldn't quit. My quiet time was anything but quiet. It's absurd, but I was beginning to think, "God, will you leave me alone so I can do my devotions without your constant interruptions?"

Finally, in exasperation, I silently shouted, "I can't bless the nations! I'm peddling as fast as I can to bless Guatemala, and I'm not even touching the surface of this tiny nation."

That's when I sensed Him say, "I'm going to give you a team." That was it. Seven words and the buzzing voice in my head quieted down. From that day on, the thought–"bless the nations"–never left me, but it had found a place of rest in my heart. It was now there as a backdrop, but no longer the loudest voice in the room.

"I'm going to give you a team." I had no idea what this team was or where they were coming from, but He said He would give me one, so I figured it was up to Him to make it happen. I was just happy that I was able to pray, able to read the Bible, and able to have my quiet time without God stepping in and messing it up. (You do see the irony in that, right?)

But His interference in my life was just beginning.

I walked a mile with Pleasure;
She chatted all the way;
But left me none the wiser
For all she had to say.

I walked a mile with Sorrow;
And ne'er a word said she;
But, oh! The things I learned from her,
When Sorrow walked with me.

- ROBERT BROWNING HAMILTON, AMERICAN POET

■ ■ ■

God whispers to us in our pleasures, speaks
to us in our conscience but shouts in our pain:
It is His megaphone to rouse a deaf world.

- C.S. LEWIS, BRITISH NOVELIST, POET
AND CHRISTIAN APOLOGIST

CHAPTER 4

Does The World Really Need Another Mom And Pop Mission Agency?

■ ■ ■

Whenever I prayed or got quiet before God, the soundtrack of "bless the nations" was still running softly in the back of my mind. But then I began to sense God asking something different from me. In my mind, this request was totally unrelated. "I want you to start a mission agency to help other people get on the mission field."

Looking back I find it hard to believe I didn't see how this fit in with "I'm going to give you a team." But clearly I'm not the sharpest marble in the deck, and I totally didn't connect the dots.

Besides, I didn't want to start a mission agency. I loved the one we were with. And Guatemala was filled with "mission agencies," many of which were individual couples, happily doing their thing. So when I first sensed God telling me to start a mission agency, I protested: "Lord, does the world really need another mom and pop mission agency? I don't think so."

I was definitely still sensitive from my Trinity World Outreach experience. But I thoroughly loved working with Missionary Ventures.

It really was a "world outreach." Plus, I got to actually work with the people, talk with the Guatemalan pastors, go into the villages, and do the work of the ministry.

Other people did all the paper pushing. Other people had to worry about budgets and administrative headaches. I got to do the fun stuff, the on-the-ground, nitty-gritty, get-your-hands-dirty ministry. But that's when the accident happened.

This Wasn't Part of My Plan

I accidentally got elected to the board of the missionary kid school in Guatemala–The Christian Academy of Guatemala. So how do you "accidentally" get elected?

My oldest son, a high schooler, knew of my love for Christian education and was concerned I would embarrass him by getting involved with the school. To assuage his fears, I promised him I would stay clear of the school. Besides, I had plenty to do without adding school duties to my plate.

However, at the annual required attendance meeting for parents, I was nominated from the floor to fill a board vacancy. I was too embarrassed to stand up and withdraw my name since my friend across the room had just nominated me. Besides, there was no way I was going to be elected.

Few people in the crowded room of over 200 parents knew me. They had more candidates than they had positions. Surely one of the better-known missionaries from one of the big agencies would win. They'd win and be happy. I'd lose and be happy. It was a win-win.

I was startled when the results came back. I was elected. How did that happen?

I decided I'd go in the next day and tell them "I prayed about it," and I wanted to be removed from the board, allowing the next person in line to take the position. The next morning, as I was on my way out the door taking the kids to school I rehearsed my "I prayed about it" speech. Then it dawned on me, if I was going to say I prayed about it, I probably should at least pray about it.

I had five minutes before I needed to leave to take the kids to school and give my speech. I ducked into a room and threw a quick prayer toward heaven. I wasn't expecting a response. I didn't even want a response. I was just "praying about it" to keep from "lying about it."

But I got a response, a quick and clear response. In my heart, I sensed God was involved in the election, and He wanted me on the board. Awk!

I KNOW EVERYTHING ABOUT LEADING YOU

I used to think one of the most difficult things about following the Lord was knowing exactly what He wanted me to do. If you're like me, you've probably said, "Lord, I'll do anything You ask if I just know for sure that it's You." And that's the rub. Is this the Lord speaking to my heart, or did I just get some bad sausage on my pizza? Is this God or indigestion?

How could Noah be so confident the Lord was telling him to build an ark? Was it an audible voice or just the quiet inner prompting that I call the voice of the Lord? How did Jesus hear which people to heal and which people to pass by–as He did at the Pool of Bethesda? How could Abraham know beyond a doubt that God was asking him to do something as off-the-charts as sacrifice his son? (There were times as a frustrated parent that I offered to do that sacrifice-your-son-thing, but I could never get a thumbs-up from heaven.)

Endless volumes have been written on how to hear from God and find His will for your life. And I've learned a lot from other writers, but it was an experience of my friend, Bill, a member of the board of Commission To Every Nation, that most changed my perspective on finding God's will.

Bill desperately needed specific direction from the Lord. He decided to get alone, pray, and fast. For three days he went into the empty sanctuary of his church, prayed, waited, listened, cried out to

God, laid on his face, read the Bible, and did everything he could to try to connect with the Lord. Finally, after three days of total divine silence, in exasperation Bill cried out, "Lord, I don't know the first thing about following You!"

It was then that he sensed a clear word in his heart. "You're right, Bill. You don't know the first thing about following Me. But I know everything about leading you."

Wow! I don't know if that statement hit Bill as hard as it impacted me when he told me the story. It rocked my world. When it came to hearing from God, I had mistakenly laid the responsibility on myself. Somehow I had to strain hard enough to wring out of the air some divine words of guidance. It was up to me to make it all happen, rather than the Father's responsibility to communicate to this dull, hard-of-hearing human being.

As a father, I realize that if I have some directions for my child, it's my responsibility to communicate clearly what I want. All my child has to do is obey, to the best of his ability, what he thinks I'm asking him to do. If there's a misunderstanding, it's my fault. I'm the adult. He's the kid. It's up to me to communicate in a way he can clearly understand.

In the same way, our Heavenly Father takes responsibility for communicating with us. He knows how simple we are. He knows what we're made of.

If He wanted a better product, He could have started with a better raw material. He made us from dirt! And we never get far from our dirty beginning. Life is quickly over, and we return to a pile of dust.

Is it possible God's inviting you to step out of your comfort cage and follow Him on an adventure? Would He lead you to do something that might not be totally safe? Would He take you down a path with an unpredictable outcome? How can you know for sure it's Him?

I don't think you can know for sure. That's where faith comes in. You move slowly and prayerfully–baby steps—trusting that even though you may not know much about following Him, He knows everything about leading you.

GOD MIGHT DESTROY YOUR REPUTATION

At the first meeting of the school board, the other board members asked me to introduce myself and tell about my background. Christian education had been such a big part of my early ministry that I couldn't avoid mentioning it. When I told them I had a Master Degree in Educational Administration and about my experience as Principal of a Christian school, a strange smirk appeared on some of their faces. I wasn't sure what was up, but it was obvious they knew something I didn't.

As the meeting progressed, I was shocked to find out that behind the scenes the school was at a crucial juncture. The board was about to replace the very loved and admired director. Though he was asked to finish out the year so they could find a replacement, once they told him of their plan, he resigned immediately.

I not only ended up on the board, but was also asked to step in as Interim Director to finish the school year. (So much for my son's desire for me to stay away from the school.)

It's probably good at this point to insert a warning. I've seen that if God's going to use you, He will sometimes start by destroying your reputation. I know that sounds strange, but He does it all the time. Jesus "made Himself of no reputation" so we shouldn't be too surprised if He does the same thing to us.[29]

To the outsider, my new responsibility as Interim Director looked like this: New guy gets elected to the board. Within a few weeks the beloved director, who has been there over 15 years, is asked to step down. Surprise! New board member smoothly slides in to take his place. Obviously this new board member is a conniver who manipulated people to get himself elected to the board so he could steal this sweet position. What a rotten guy. He pushes his way in and immediately casts the beloved director aside like an old sock.

Surely that's how it appeared, and there was nothing I could do to convince folks otherwise. I didn't even want to be on the board. God set me up!

Sometimes God's work in your life will cause the casual observer to make harsh judgments about you. And you find yourself in a position where you can't defend yourself. You have to leave it to the Lord.

Why didn't Gabriel appear to Mary when she was sitting with her friends around the city well? No one would have doubted her fantastic story. She would have been the town heroine. He could have at least appeared when her parents were present so they would have believed her. Joseph, too, had a private experience with no witnesses, and just like that, their hard-earned reputations were instantly ruined.

Noah looked like a fool. David was shamefully chased out of Jerusalem by his own son. The great John the Baptist died an ignoble death in prison. The highly educated and well-respected Saul of Tarsus became "the scum of the earth, the refuse of the world," when God grabbed hold of him.[30]

Count the cost. When God uses you, He often requires you to sacrifice your reputation on the altar. Friends, family, the church, even strangers may misjudge your motives and accuse you of all sorts of crazy things. His prophets and even His Son were slandered. Why are we surprised when it happens to us? If we're going to be used by God, we've got to be more concerned about what He says on "that day" than what people say on this day.

My accidental board membership was definitely God ordered. As Interim Director I led the school through what could have been a very painful and divisive time for the entire missions community. But God was working this for my good as well. The event that impacted my future most was the application of a Methodist teacher.

OK, Lord, I Guess You're Right (again)

Like most MK (Missionary Kid) schools, the Christian Academy of Guatemala is almost always critically short of teachers–often to a point of desperation. A major reason for this is that the teachers aren't paid. To keep tuition low enough that missionaries can send their children, all teachers are asked to raise their own support, just like most of the missionaries they serve.

We had a highly qualified teacher apply. She recently retired and her pension would allow her to live well in Guatemala. We had cleared the biggest hurdle—funding. Now we just needed an agency that could sponsor her. At the time, the Methodist church didn't have any missionaries in Guatemala, so she couldn't come with them.

The Baptist missionary on the board said, "We'd love to send her, but she isn't Baptist." The Assemblies of God and the Lutheran missionaries had the same response. One independent agency was willing to send her, but they charged an 18% administrative fee, which meant she would have to raise support above her pension just to cover administrative costs for this mission. She wasn't willing to do that.

We couldn't find a way to get this teacher to Guatemala. I couldn't believe it! We lost a highly qualified and desperately needed teacher.

Rather sheepishly I had to admit, "OK, Lord, I guess You're right (again). Maybe the world does need another mom and pop mission agency. One that can help ordinary people who are called, are needed, and are willing to go, but may not fit the traditional missionary or denominational molds."

I could see there was a need for another agency, but I still didn't want to be the guy to start it. I loved what I was doing and didn't want to change.

I-Don't-Want-To-Obey Obedience

That's when the urging in my heart–that nudging from the Holy Spirit—changed. It had been a gentle voice, "Bless the nations—start a mission agency—I'll give you a team." But now I sensed that voice shift from a gentle invitation to a stern question, "Are you going to obey Me or not?" It was no longer the dove of the Holy Spirit speaking. I was facing the Lion of the Tribe of Judah, and He wanted an answer.

I've found the Lord is very patient with us when we're trying to discover His plan. He will do whatever it takes to make it clear in a way we can understand. He'll speak from a burning bush, the mouth of a donkey, or through an accidental election. But once we know what He wants, He expects obedience. Once we know, only a total fool disobeys.

"I guess I'm going to start another mom and pop mission agency. But, Lord, that doesn't mean I have to like it."

Like a spoiled child who eats his broccoli but whines and pouts with every bite, I fussed, "OK, I'll do what's necessary to start this thing, but I'm not going to do anything to make it grow." It wasn't so much a response of rebellion as one of hopelessness.

I tried everything I knew to make Trinity World Outreach grow into a real world outreach, and it was a dismal failure. Obviously I didn't have what it took to build some big ministry. Why waste any more of my life trying to do something I was totally incapable of?

I'm not advocating this type of communication with the Lord. I marvel that He didn't "send me to my room without any dinner." But since He knows my heart anyway, I've always felt I might as well be honest with Him. David, Gideon, Moses, and others all honestly expressed their doubts, fears and frustrations with God. Our honesty doesn't intimidate Him.

And the most amazing thing is this: God honors "I-don't-want-to-do-it" obedience. Gideon was terrified. Moses pleaded to not be sent back to Egypt. And it may astound you to realize that even Jesus didn't always want to obey!

In the garden He made it clear He didn't want to go to the cross. At the end of His prayer, He hadn't changed His mind. He said, "Not my will but Yours be done." That's Bible talk for, "This is not what I want to do but I will do it because it's what You want done."

Obedience is a Choice, Not a Feeling

Sometimes God will ask us to do things we don't want to do. It may be because it seems so trivial–"Don't leave that shopping cart in the middle of the parking lot." It might be because we can't see a reason for it–"Does the world really need another mom and pop mission agency?" It might be because we're afraid and feel inadequate. "Quit your job, raise support, and follow Me onto the mission field."

I'm so glad God honors our obedience even if we don't feel like obeying. Many times I can't control my feelings. I can't get them to agree with God. But I can choose to obey even when I don't feel like it.

I can choose to love when I don't feel like loving.
I can choose to forgive when I don't feel like forgiving.
I can choose to be kind when I don't feel like being kind.
I can choose to be patient when I don't feel like being patient.
God honors the person who obeys even if he doesn't feel like it.

But here's the most precious part. When we obey, often our feelings will get in line. It's much easier to behave our way into feeling correctly than to feel our way into behaving correctly. God honors obedience. If you want to be a person that God does extraordinary things through, this is a key—obey.

Obey when you're afraid to.
Obey when you don't feel like it.
Obey when it doesn't make sense.
Obey when you can't see the reason for it.
Just obey.

I would obey the Lord, but I knew there was no way this mom and pop agency was going to fulfill what He seemed to be telling me He wanted done–bless the nations. Blessing the nations would take some big ministry with lots of people and lots of money.

The leaders of big ministries were charismatic, talented people driven by a clear vision. They were high energy and knew how to motivate others to rush into battle and take the hill regardless of the cost. They were like those officers I was surrounded by on the admiral's staff in the Navy—gifted, driven, amazing leaders. And then there was me, a very ordinary enlisted guy.

I didn't have what it took to "bless the nations." There was no dazzling five-year vision or awe-inspiring mission statement. I wasn't a charismatic, driven leader who could motivate people to sacrifice all for the cause. Quite obviously God had the wrong guy.

But what do you do when you think God has called you to do the impossible? You start by doing what you can do. You start by doing the possible and then leave the rest with Him. I could file the paperwork for a 501(c)(3) non-profit with the government. I could do that, but I had no false hopes that this tiny mom and pop agency would ever become a team that would bless the nations.

And that teacher we needed at the Christian Academy of Guatemala had already accepted another offer, so she was gone. I only knew one other couple that had ever expressed an interest in missions. I could talk to them, but that was the extent of what I could do. After that I planned to check "obey" off my list and get back to real life. If God wanted another mom and pop agency, I'd do my part to give Him one.

Often the interruptions of our agenda
are God's insertions of His agenda.

- RICK MALM

■   ■   ■

God guides us, despite our uncertainties and
our vagueness, even through our failings and
mistakes... He leads us step-by-step, from event
to event. Only afterwards, as we look back over
the way we have come... do we experience the
feeling of having been led without knowing it, the
feeling that God has mysteriously guided us.

- PAUL TOURNIER, SWISS AUTHOR AND PHYSICIAN

CHAPTER 5

That'll Never Work

■ ■ ■

COMMISSION TO EVERY NATION WAS originally called T.E.A.M. Missions. T.E.A.M. was an acronym for "Together Everyone Accomplishes More." My kids tell me acronyms are cheesy. That's probably true, but I've always loved cheese.

I chose the name for two reasons. First of all, because of what the Lord said about giving me a team to bless the nations. And, second, because the state of Texas rejected every other name I submitted. It seemed like there was already a corporation with the same name or one very similar to every one I thought of.

In desperation I had submitted some rather exotic names and all were rejected so I was pretty sure a simple name like T.E.A.M. Missions didn't have a chance. But on December 23, 1994, we received an early Christmas present. The state of Texas approved the name T.E.A.M. Missions and the adventure began.

Apparently Texas, like me, had never heard of The Evangelical Alliance Mission (T.E.A.M.), which was already over one hundred years old when we were just starting. It wouldn't be long, however, before T.E.A.M. and T.E.A.M. Missions would meet.

I had no great vision of T.E.A.M. Missions becoming some huge mission agency, yet at the same time, God had started this whole thing by saying He wanted to bless the nations. What if it really happened? What if God did something crazy and this thing did explode to have a global impact?

I was skeptical, but I knew we should lay a solid foundation just in case God did go wild. The seeds of the destruction of a ministry often lie in compromises or shortcuts taken when laying the foundation of that ministry. I wanted to follow Paul's pattern of "taking pains to do what is right, not only in the eyes of the Lord but also in the eyes of man." [31]

Can We Trust Missionaries?

A chance meeting led to a highly qualified Christian CPA, who also had a background in law, volunteering to help us get organized. He offered to do it totally free, which miraculously was exactly what we could afford. As I laid out the plan, he listened patiently and then gave his evaluation, "That'll never work."

He was referring to my desire to charge no "administrative fee" for T.E.A.M. Missionaries. Instead, I wanted to send 100% of the donated funds to the missionary. Then, like a church that's dependent upon the tithes of its members, I felt we should let the missionaries pray and voluntarily send back to the mission the percentage they felt God said they should give. This voluntary "tithe" would fund the mission to serve all of us–myself included, since I was going to continue to raise full support for my family.

I admit it was a crazy idea, and I thought my CPA friend was probably right: "That'll never work." Because, for it to work, every missionary would have to be obedient and generous. Otherwise the "obedient and generous" would end up funding the costs of the "disobedient and cheap."

Could we really trust missionaries to hear from God, respond in obedience, and be generous? What a question. If we can't trust them to be faithful with money, why would we think we could trust them with real riches–the great treasure of the gospel? I felt we should at least give it a try and see what happened.

The Wisdom of Godly Counsel

I believe in godly counsel. Solomon, the wisest man who ever lived, said more about the wisdom of seeking counsel than any other Biblical writer. If Solomon needed it, I certainly do, too.

But, there are times the Lord will lead you past the point where wise counsel says, "That'll never work." He will lead you to step out of the boat, leave the normal path, and walk with Him.

In Matthew 14, the disciples were crossing the lake when Jesus came toward them walking on water. He invited Peter to join Him on the waves. Imagine if Peter had called a meeting to discuss the wisdom of this proposal.

"I heard the Lord call me to jump out of this boat and go to Him. What do you think?"

We can guess the responses.

"Don't be silly. Why would you want to do that?"

"There's so much noise from the wind and the waves, how can you be sure you were called to go?"

"Don't do anything crazy. Just wait in the boat. If it's really Him, He'll be here in a few minutes."

"Why would you want to leave? We need you here. Just stay with us."

But Peter heard an invitation. He chose to follow that voice, not knowing what would happen. With no promise of success and contrary to all common sense, he stepped out in obedience. He left the safety of the boat and the company of family and friends to go with the Lord.

And how'd that work out for him?

Things went OK at first.
But then he saw the obstacles - the wind and the waves.
He got terrified and began to sink.

Maybe he should have stayed in the boat.
Maybe he had missed God.
But then the Lord reached out and rescued him.

Yes, he got soaking wet in front of all of his friends.
But did he fail? Should he have stayed in the boat?
It's true that all his buddies who stayed behind stayed dry, but...

But Peter walked on water!
He was soaked and almost sank, but instead, he stood.
The Lord, who is able, made him stand.
And he experienced the miraculous.
God had come through, and Peter walked on water!

I guarantee none of the dry guys in the boat laughed at him for courageously stepping out. They had seen the miraculous. They had seen God lift him up. They had seen an ordinary man do the extraordinary because he followed the Lord's invitation.

There were some terrifying moments, but he experienced something amazing–he walked on water! Was it worth it? I sure think a few moments of terror and a little water in my sandals would be a small price to pay to experience something no other human being had ever experienced.

The Importance of Following The Lord's Invitation

When you follow the Lord's invitation there may be terrifying moments. In fact, if there isn't a little terror, you probably need to dream bigger. If you can accomplish the dream without God's help, then it isn't a God-sized dream. "Impossible without Him" is the hallmark stamped on every dream from God.

When you follow the Lord's invitation, there may be times you wonder if you really heard Him. I've never been able to say without a doubt that God was leading me to do this or do that. There is always some question, some insecurity. That's what keeps me from charging ahead. It keeps my ear tuned to hear the Shepherd's voice. It keeps me moving slowly, carefully, and prayerfully.

When you follow the Lord's invitation, you may face obstacles. It may seem the wind and waves are going to overwhelm you, and you're going down. In fact, "if you have no opposition in the place you serve, you are serving in the wrong place."[32]

But remember, this was God's idea. It was His dream. He just invited you to come along. He will surely lift you up as a trophy of his ability to make you stand.

When you follow the Lord's invitation, you may appear foolish. Of course the world will think you're crazy, and often, even God's people will question your sanity. It happened to Moses when he returned with a dream to deliver God's people. It happened to David when he offered to defend God's name against Goliath.

Those who haven't heard the Lord's invitation can't understand. They can't be expected to understand. What sort of fool stands up to Pharaoh with a rod? What sort of fool attacks a trained warrior with only a sling? What sort of fool tries to walk on water? What sort of fool leaves home, family, friends, career, country, culture, and everything familiar to step into the unknown?

Peter took a risk. "What's going to happen when my feet hit the water? What if the Lord doesn't come through? What if I didn't hear him correctly? What if I fail? What if I look foolish?" If Peter insisted on having all the answers before he left the boat, he would have never experienced the adventure of a lifetime.

The Importance of Risk

If I insist on playing it safe, being in control, and knowing what's going to happen when I step into obedience, I'll never obey. I'll never leave the boat. I'll miss the adventure with my Lord.

Because God's not going to give me those answers ahead of time. If He did, He'd remove the risk, He'd remove the faith. Where there's no risk there's no faith. Risk and faith go hand-in-hand.

Seeking and submitting to godly counsel should be our default setting, but there are times when the Divine Counselor will instruct us to go beyond all other counsel and venture with Him into the unknown. He invites us to join Him in doing something "that'll never work."

That's not to say we throw ourselves off the pinnacle of the temple just to see if the angels catch us. I'm not talking about putting the Lord to some foolish test that we come up with. I'm talking about obeying the voice of the Great Counselor when we sense Him saying to do something contrary to all other counsel.

So how can I tell when I should listen to wise counsel and when I should step out of the boat and trust God to do the miraculous? How do I know if I am acting on faith or presumption?

Sometimes it's simple to know the difference. Is this your idea–something you dreamed up that you think would help God? Or do you sense God saying it's something you should do? Good idea or God idea?

Jesus said, "Come." Peter obeyed. Faith is obeying God's voice and doing as He instructs even if it makes no sense. Presumption is deciding what I think is a good idea or what I think should happen and trying to force God to come through for me.

I certainly didn't think starting a mission was a good idea. But the Lord convinced me it was a God idea. Was giving 100% to the missionary a good idea or a God idea? Frankly, I wasn't sure. And sometimes–most of the time–you can't be sure.

Following wise and godly counsel is a Biblical principle, but there are other Biblical principles as well. The idea of giving "what you have decided in your heart to give, not reluctantly or under compulsion" was a Biblical principle that worked for the church.[33] Could it work for a para-church organization?

I felt it was worth a try even though I couldn't say with 100% certainty it was an imperative from the Lord. And since we were already way beyond my comfort zone we might as well go totally crazy and try to follow Biblically established funding principles as well. We would let the missionaries–assuming we ever had any besides my family–give "what (they) decided in (their) hearts to give, not reluctantly or under compulsion".

And what if I was wrong?

It wouldn't be the first time. God is gracious and most decisions are not irreversible. If you feel the Lord has told you to do something that exceeds wise counsel's advice, give it a try. You may face some moments of pure terror, but you may also walk on water. You may find that God transforms your greatest mess into your greatest message.

We weren't sure if we could make it as missionaries when we first moved to Guatemala. What if we failed? Neither Jana nor I are the adventurous, "live-on-the-ragged-edge" types. We couldn't even "count the cost" because there were more unknowns than knowns involved.

All we could do was obey, to the best of our ability, what we sensed God was inviting us to do, and from there, trust that He would hold us up and get us through. All we could do was step into the water and see what happened next.

Avoiding Analysis Paralysis

Those who feel they must know every outcome, every possibility, every step of the journey before they start, will never begin. Analysis paralysis will enslave them to false security. They'll pass through life in a cocoon, never knowing what might have been if they had stretched their wings to soar.

They may arrive safely at heaven's gates, but they'll arrive dry. They'll have no stories of epic terror but neither will they have stories of epic triumphs. Their experiences of walking with God will contain only tales of paltry victories and answers to petty prayers.

President Theodore Roosevelt spoke of these "poor spirits" when he said: "Far better is it to dare mighty things, to win glorious triumphs, even though checkered by failure... than to rank with those poor spirits who neither enjoy nor suffer much, because they live in a gray twilight that knows not victory nor defeat."[34]

You can't let the "what ifs" keep you restrained safely in the boat, because you cannot possibly predict what will happen when you obey. Obedience sets in motion supernatural elements that cause the equation to no longer add up. Obedience results in five loaves feeding five thousand with twelve baskets of leftovers. It results in seven loaves feeding four thousand with seven baskets of leftovers.[35]

Let me say that another way: when God's kids obey, crazy things start to happen. Things you can't anticipate or plan for—water gets firm enough to walk on, seas and rivers part revealing dry ground, prison doors open, and God glorifies his name through unqualified, ordinary people. Step out. Obey God. Watch what He does in response.

"SMALL" SOUNDS GOOD TO ME

As I continued to explain the 100%-goes-to-the-missionary-and-we-voluntarily-give-back-to-enable-the-mission-to-serve-us-all plan to my new CPA friend he admitted, "Well, it might work if you stay very small."

That sounded great because that's exactly what I expected. We would stay "very small"–my family and maybe a couple of other folks. After all, I was planning to stay in Guatemala, working with the pastors and churches there. I wasn't going to recruit or even tell folks about this new venture—except, of course, those who were part of our support team–our prayer and financial donors.

At that time, there were no websites, no online marketing, no email, and few cell phones. We didn't even receive mail at our home in Guatemala, so there was no way for people to conveniently contact us. There was really no possibility that this was going to grow as long as my family stayed safely secluded in Guatemala.

As far as overhead expenses we missionaries had to cover, a garage-type room in my home in Guatemala was going to be our

International Headquarters. In evenings and on weekends, I would be the bookkeeper. This was a concern because my college accounting grades clearly showed I had no business doing this. But a friend set me up with a computer checkbook that he assured me was a "no brainer"– which perfectly fit my level of accounting skills.

A volunteer in Texas was going to go to the post office each week and fax me a photocopy of any checks that came in. Another volunteer was going to make the bank deposit each week. The word "internet" was not in our vocabulary, so we had no online banking. Each month I would be faxed a copy of the bank statement so I could reconcile it with our no-brainer checkbook program.

All receipting would be done from Guatemala using the Guatemalan mail system. It was rather unreliable but it was cheap, and cheap was the priority. Each donor would get a receipt and a thank you note in one of those thin, exotic looking airmail envelopes with the red, white and blue lines around the edges. It would come complete with Guatemalan postage stamps.

Our first upgrade in this donor management system came when I received a note from a friend. Nancy wrote, "I know this sounds pathetically lazy, but could you include a return envelope with the receipt? It just makes it so much easier for me to send the next gift."

I bought a box of blank envelopes, invested in a return address rubber stamp and began hand stamping each envelope that went in with the receipts. In those pre-internet, pre-cell phone, pre-everybody-over-the-age-of-2-has-a-computer days, this was a pretty high-tech operation complete with a thermal fax machine and now the ability to "print" our own return envelopes.

We would be dependent upon any future missionaries to be faithful to support the ministry so T.E.A.M. Missions could help them like it was doing for us, but the costs were so low we figured that shouldn't be a problem–as long as we stayed "very small."

T.E.A.M. Missions was up and running with a well-oiled group of volunteers and a flawless receipting system. But to be fully obedient to the Lord's command to start a mission agency, I needed to do one more thing. Then I could settle back into my own personal mission ministry routine and put this whole "bless the nations" thing behind me.

I knew of one couple–just one–who might be interested in joining the team of my wife and me. I planned a trip back to the US to meet with them. Perhaps they would be our first, and probably only, team members.

We can afford to follow Him to
failure. Faith dares to fail.

- A.W. TOZER, AMERICAN PASTOR AND AUTHOR

■ ■ ■

One half hour before the flight
Still a fool was Orville Wright.

- BURT ROSENBERG, JOY SPRITZER-IN-
CHIEF AT ROSENBERG MINISTRIES

NOTE: Commission To Every Nation complies with the seven standards of
responsible stewardship put forth by the Evangelical Council for Financial
Accountability (ECFA) of which CTEN is a member and, as per US tax
codes, it retains full discretion and control over all gifts given to the mission.

CHAPTER 6

Is There A Place For Me In Missions?

■ ■ ■

THEY WERE KNOWN IN THEIR church as the mission folks. They talked excitedly about how one day they would be missionaries. Whenever people found out I was a missionary, they asked if I knew this couple. So we set up a meeting, and I told them how they could finally fulfill their dream to be missionaries. They could be part of T.E.A.M. Missions, and I would help them find a place to serve.

To my surprise they immediately started backpedaling with half a dozen excuses. I felt like I was living Jesus' story in Luke 14 where a man prepares a feast and invites all his friends.

"'Come, for all things are now ready.' But they all began making excuses."

I quickly realized it wasn't just a timing issue. These were nice folks who loved the *idea* of missions, but they weren't going to actually change their lives, step out of the boat, and go anywhere as missionaries.

I could relate. In most Christian circles, being "missions-minded" is cool and admirable. Talking about how important mission work is produces knowing nods of approval. But becoming a missionary is a huge, terrifying step into the unknown. Most of us love the *idea* of missions like all the mice in the popular children's story loved the *idea* of putting a bell around the cat's neck. "It's a great idea! I am all for it as long as it's you, not me, doing it."

THREE STRIKES BUT NOT OUT

These were the only people I knew in the whole world who might be interested in going as missionaries and they were running like scared mice–clearly saying, "No! Absolutely not."

Apparently T.E.A.M. Missions was destined to be a failure just like Trinity World Outreach. T.E.A.M. Missions would be a "mom and pop" organization with a big sounding name. Jana and I were going to be the whole "team."

But my sure-fire-yes candidates who were disappearing in a cloud of dust had brought another couple with them that evening. The husband, a quiet guy, timidly interjected a question.

"I'm not very smart, but I can work hard. Is there a place for me in missions?"

I'm pretty sure it took a lot of courage for him to ask that question. Ellis and Betty were simple, quiet folks. The closest thing they had to missionary experience was visiting Oklahoma. Other than that, they'd never been out of Texas. (Texans understand that visiting Oklahoma counts as foreign missions experience.)

They had no college, no Bible school, and no special training or skills. He was a fence builder for ranchers. She was a stay-at-home mom. They were untrained—strike one. They had never been out of the country, even on a short-term trip. They had no experience–strike 2. They had two teenage children at home. Most agencies I know wouldn't consider sending first time missionaries with kids that age. Strike three. They were out–totally unqualified.

Except for one thing. And that one thing is something I'm 100% convinced is the most important thing–they were willing.

Ellis was asking if there was a place for him in missions. Suddenly I felt like the dog that chased cars, caught one, and didn't know what to do with it. We had our first T.E.A.M. Missions volunteers, but I had no idea what to do with them.

I didn't know anything about them, and I didn't have an official-looking application for them to fill out. I didn't know what they could do or wanted to do. I didn't have a ministry location lined up for them.

Most agencies have established hoops for the applicant to jump through. "Do these ten, twenty, or fifty things, and we'll know you're qualified." But we didn't need that. We already knew they *weren't* qualified. So what would we do now?

I had known and admired Ellis' pastor for years, so I decided to start there. I'd talk with Keith and see what Ellis and Betty had been doing at their church. "Surely," I thought, "they've been serving. I'll see what kind of job they did there. If they haven't been serving in their local church, why would we send them to another country to serve?"

It made sense, but what I didn't realize was I had just created a hoop for someone to jump through–you must have served in your local church. But certainly that's a good hoop. No one could criticize that requirement.

How To Build A Missionary Obstacle Course

But that's how missionary obstacle courses evolve–one logical barrier at a time. We add this good requirement, that great idea, another splendid criteria, and before long we have a zillion roadblocks–all good and reasonable–that a candidate must hurdle before they can answer the Lord's invitation to missions.

Our efforts at missions mobilization often end in immobilization because of the obstacles we erect, a condition I refer to as "Preparation Paralysis." We mean well, but these endless barriers are part of the reason "the harvest is plentiful, but the workers are few."[36]

I talked with their pastor. Keith spoke highly of their character. They were a good, down-to-earth, hard-working family. He was 100% behind them going as missionaries. They faithfully attended the church and the church would support them spiritually and financially. They had his highest recommendation, but I discovered they had never served in the church.

What was I to do now? If their own pastor was totally supportive, could I really disqualify them because of a barrier I came up with? It wasn't written in stone on Mt Sinai. I realized that as soon as they expressed a desire to go, I began to erect barriers–not to protect them, but to protect me. By default I basically said, "No, you can't go unless...."

And right there I learned a couple of things that would tremendously impact the future of the ministry.

1. Policies are where we start thinking, not where we stop thinking.
2. Our default answer must be "Yes," not "No."

POLICIES ARE WHERE WE START THINKING

People come from such unique situations and circumstances that even reasonable barriers can become unreasonable and eliminate great people. Obviously we need policies. But policies can easily replace common sense and initiative.

Policies tend to shut down thinking. If I do something contrary to policy, I can be reprimanded. But, if I'm following company policy, even if what I do is clearly boneheaded, I'm safe.

Policies should be where we start thinking, not where we stop thinking. When we hit a policy roadblock, we need to apply common sense and spirit-empowered wisdom. We also need to apply some faith.

Look at the individuals and the situation to decide if the policy fits or if it needs to be waived in order to accomplish the primary objective of the organization. And never forget that if it is God calling them, then He will enable them to stand. He will accomplish His good pleasure through them, regardless of how unqualified they may be by our standards.

Policies should be like the Sabbath, "made to meet the needs of people and not people to meet the requirements of the policy."[37] Individuals, in all their marvelous diversity, must take priority. Thanks to our willingness to look at each person as an individual and bend policies to fit people rather than requiring people fit the policy, we have discovered that exceptions often turn out to be exceptional. Those who don't fit the mold often were created by God from a different mold to meet a different need.

So, while we normally look to see how someone has been serving in his or her local church, that's not a barrier that would keep someone from going with Commission To Every Nation. And we approach all our policies with that same "written in sand not written in stone" attitude.

People are different. Churches are different. Circumstances are different. And who is the Creator of all this diversity? If God chooses to fashion each and every snowflake, hair on our head, and person uniquely, why do we insist on creating uniform boxes to shove them into? There are places in God's kingdom for round pegs, square pegs, pegs that defy description, and even non-pegs.

Individual consideration, common sense, and above all, listening to the Spirit of the Lord, must have first priority. If it's evident someone is responding to the Lord's command to go, then we need to do everything we can to help them go. Our unique, one-of-a-kind God loves to do unique things with unique people.

Only one man walked on water. Only one killed a giant with a sling. Only one destroyed an army with torches and trumpets. Only one built an ark. Jesus healed one with a touch, another with a word, and one poor fellow got a mud ball rubbed in his blind eyes. On and on the one-of-a-kind stories could go. Each happened because someone was listening to God and took a step that was contrary to good policy.

OUR DEFAULT ANSWER MUST BE "YES"

I also determined that when someone applied to go as a missionary, our default answer would be "Yes."

Like my initial response to Ellis and Betty, "No, you can't go unless...", in most areas of life, our default response is, "No." If a parent isn't sure about a request, they say, "No." "No, you can't go. No, you can't do that."

In Guatemala, I asked a government official if I could renew my visa with a color photo instead of a black and white photo. You could tell by his expression that he had no idea and immediately I knew what he would say —"No." Later I discovered that either was perfectly acceptable, but "no" was safe. It carried no responsibility and no risk for him.

"No" almost never means, "I've considered your request, looked at the options, and here's my decision." No is just the safe answer.

It can work that way in missions, too. I can't know for sure if you'll be a successful missionary. What if you get hurt? What if things go badly? What if you mess up and embarrass the mission or damage our reputation? What if you fail and leave the field early? If I say "yes," I take a risk. "No," is safe and so it easily becomes our default. The missionary applicant starts at "No" and has to work hard to earn a "Yes."

"No, you can't go unless... unless you meet these fifty prerequisites."

I determined our default answer would be, "Yes. Yes, you can go unless... unless you work hard to prove you shouldn't go."

Unless you convince us otherwise, we're going to believe you can do this because "The one who calls you is faithful, and He will do it." "Yes you can go, and we believe you 'will stand, for the Lord is able to make (you) stand.'"[38]

"Yes" is a risky answer. But where there's no risk, there's no faith. Where there's no risk, there's no need for God. "Yes" risks the glorious. "Yes" invites God to step in and do extraordinary things. We default to "yes" because that's the only way to help ordinary people partner with God to accomplish the extraordinary.

So policies are where we start thinking, not where we stop thinking, and our default answer is, "Yes!" Our goal is to minimize barriers and maximize workers in response to the heart cry of Jesus: "...Pray to the Lord who is in charge of the harvest; ask Him to send more workers into his fields."[39]

That's why we have only two primary qualifications–a letter of recommendation and a letter of invitation.

LETTER OF RECOMMENDATION

We can't possibly know each applicant nor get to know them adequately in an interview, through a barrage of testing, or even through a long application process. We look to someone who has known and observed them over a period of time. Usually a pastor is an ideal choice, but even that policy must remain flexible.

In this diverse world of ours, there are legitimate reasons a person may not be close enough to a pastor to get a helpful recommendation. And pastors are imperfect people, just like all of us. So normally we require a "glowing" pastoral recommendation, but that policy is the place we start thinking, not where we stop thinking. The spirit of the rule is to find a reliable person with spiritual insight who can personally vouch for the applicant's integrity and walk with the Lord.

There is a place for reasonable policies and procedures, but they must always remain subservient to common sense and fulfilling the vision for which the Lord brought the organization into existence. God formed T.E.A.M. Missions (later Commission To Every Nation) to send a team to bless the nations. If we ever begin to limit that purpose, God will establish another agency that will fully obey and fulfill His dream.

Our default must remain, "Yes."

LETTER OF INVITATION

Ellis and Betty were both excitedly volunteering to follow the Lord, so I asked Ellis what he wanted to do as a missionary. He replied, "I've always liked agriculture. Is there a farm I could work on?"

Remember our wonderful home school teacher who was snatched away from us by the dashing young agricultural missionary? He owed me one. Mike did agricultural work in the remote Mayan village of Nebaj, Quiche, in Guatemala. I knew he was an extremely busy guy because he was also starting Bible schools to help pastors in even more remote villages. I didn't know if he would have time to mess with a new family who couldn't speak Spanish and had no experience or training.

When I called, I couldn't believe his response. He majored in agriculture in college for the purpose of being an agricultural missionary. Now he was getting so busy training pastors that he'd been praying for someone to come help with the agricultural work. This was an answer to prayer for him and for us!

But immediately I had another concern. Mike was a friend. I wanted him to stay a friend. What if, in spite of the glowing report from their pastor, Ellis and Betty turned out to be a burden instead of a blessing?

I decided they'd come for a trial visit, work with Mike, and then return home. If Mike wanted them back, he would send me a letter inviting them to come and explaining what they would do. That way, if something went wrong I could remind him, "You asked for them."

GOD'S BEEN BUSY AT WORK IN YOUR LIFE

I wish I could claim our two criteria for qualifying missionaries–letter of recommendation and letter of invitation–came through intense times of prayer, but now you know the truth. I needed someone who knew the applicant and could vouch for their integrity. Their pastor seemed like a reasonable choice. And I wanted to let myself off the hook in case these new missionaries ended up creating problems.

Surely, somewhere in Proverbs it says, "God looks out for the simple." Just like there have been times the Lord orchestrated circumstances to destroy my reputation, I've seen Him arrange other situations that made me look like a genius. But I realize it doesn't have anything to do with me. He just has a soft spot in His heart for missions, missionaries, and simple people who will obey Him—even if reluctantly.

I was amazed at how God orchestrated the placement of our first missionary couple. He loves to do things in a way that turns out to be a double blessing. We were providing an answer to a missionary's prayer for desperately needed help, and just as amazingly, we were taking an ordinary couple and helping them walk into the extraordinary things God wanted to do through them.

Ever notice how God is always working behind the scenes, ordering everything according to His perfect timing? I guarantee God has been at work behind the scenes in your life, too. What are the skills he's given you? What are you good at or what do you really like to do? Before He formed you, He had a plan for you. He has been overseeing the experiences of your life to prepare you and He's been working elsewhere creating the place where you'll fit perfectly and be able to bring Him glory.

And guess what? When you're bold enough to take the first step, as simple as it might be, He will delight you by doing greater things than you imagined possible. That's what happened with Ellis and Betty.

They spent a week with Mike, and he enthusiastically invited them to come back full time and serve the Mayan people of Nebaj. But could an untrained, unqualified couple really get people to believe in them enough to support them financially? More surprises and lessons lay ahead for us all.

All God's giants have been weak men who
did great things for God because they
reckoned on God being with them.

- HUDSON TAYLOR, MISSIONARY TO CHINA AND
FOUNDER OF THE CHINA INLAND MISSION

■ ■ ■

A Ditty About the Pity That Workers are Few.

The harvest is plentiful,
but the barriers are, too.
Perhaps that's the reason
the workers are few.

We pray for more workers,
but once they commit
We quickly find reasons
to call them unfit.

My people, like sheep,
are helpless, harassed.
They need caring shepherds
Not theology class.

I'll choose who I send
By checking their heart.
I don't need the rich
or the strong or the smart.

I simply need servants
Who'll trust and obey.
Who are willing to follow
And do what I say.

My plan is to see
My kingdom advance.
And I'll make it happen.
Just give folks a chance.

A chance to fail.
Or perhaps to soar.
A chance to discover
What I created them for.

– RICK MALM

■ ■ ■

When he saw the crowds, he had compassion on
them, because they were harassed and helpless,
like sheep without a shepherd. Then he said to his
disciples, "The harvest is plentiful but the workers
are few. Ask the Lord of the harvest, therefore,
to send out workers into his harvest field."

– MATTHEW 9:36-38

CHAPTER 7

I've Just Been Waiting For You To Ask

■ ■ ■

WITHIN TWO YEARS, T.E.A.M. MISSIONS had grown to ten mission-ary families. I couldn't understand it. I wasn't doing anything to make it grow.

How were these people hearing about us? This was before web-sites and internet marketing. We didn't have a U.S. phone number that people could call. We weren't doing anything to find new missionaries to join the team.

But God was sending folks our way who wanted to go into the mission field. Some had hit roadblocks. Some were already serving, but a God-inspired change in ministry focus left them without a mission agency to partner with them.

One couple had been sent by their home church, so when the church experienced a painful split, it could no longer help them admin-istratively, but it was still behind them spiritually. Their letter, mailed from the Philippines, miraculously reached our home in Guatemala. I could sense their pain as I read, "It's lonely being out here on our own. Can we join T.E.A.M. Missions?"

Another couple came to us because a group of Guatemalan pastors asked the husband to use his PhD in cross-cultural ministry to start a school to train Guatemalans to go as missionaries. "We can teach them the Bible," these pastors explained, "but we need someone to prepare them to go cross-culturally." Guatemalan missionaries funded by Guatemalan churches sent to other countries as cross-cultural missionaries. How cool is that?

His U.S. based agency thought it was totally cool. They fully supported the idea, but... but it was outside the bounds of their vision. He was told he would have to find another agency to help him fulfill the dream of these Latin American pastors.

One couple asked to join T.E.A.M. Missions after they called the international director of their current mission for advice. The director responded, "You're where? In Oaxaca, Mexico? I didn't know we had missionaries in Oaxaca." The husband told me they wanted to join because, "We just want to know someone knows we're here and is praying for us."

WHY MAKE IT HARDER THAN IT ALREADY IS?

Some of our first T.E.A.M. Missionaries were already serving on the field. Others had hit hurdles that disqualified them in the eyes of traditional mission agencies. There are a thousand reasons to say, "No."

You're too old. You're too young. You have too many children. Your children aren't the right ages. You don't have seminary training. You don't have pastoral experience. You don't have the personality necessary to raise your support. You have a low aptitude for language learning. We don't send anyone who has been divorced. We don't send singles. We don't have anyone working in that area, and we only send teams.

Why do so many mission agencies make it so hard for people to go? Aren't there already plenty of hurdles? Why create even more?

Recently I was talking with a man who used to be responsible for training new missionaries within his agency. He explained that they chose the hardest location possible for their training base. "Most missionaries would never face the hardships they faced living at the remote base we used for training." He explained that the leaders of the mission felt, "If they can make it there, they can make it anywhere."

I was baffled. Really? I find that logic abhorrent. What about those who can't make it there but who could do amazing things in any of ten thousand other places? Why make it harder than it already is?

Apparently they eventually made it hard enough that this trainer chose to leave too. When I met him, he was applying to stay in the same country and serve under Commission To Every Nation.

There Is A Place For Everyone

The Marines used to say they were "the few, the proud." That's a great slogan for the Marines, but it's a lousy one for God's kingdom. We should be doing all we can to encourage the weaker-but-willing missionaries instead of trying to crush them. The job of world evangelism is far too big to be left to "the few." We need the Marines (speaking metaphorically), but we also need the Army, Navy, Air Force, Coast Guard, Merchant Marines, Boy Scouts, Girls Scouts, Cub Scouts, Brownies and all who are willing to go. My point is, there is a place for you!

God kept sending willing people to join T.E.A.M. Missions. Within two years, ten families had joined. I couldn't believe how big we had grown. I distinctly remember the day in 1996 when I realized this thing I didn't want to do, this thing I saw no need for, this helping-other-people-join-us-on-the-mission-field thing was getting serious. "Lord, I love what we're doing here in Guatemala. I love working with the people and with the pastors. I love the culture, the language, and oh, yes, the food. But I also see that for me to be of any real help to these folks that you've obviously sent our way, I need to return to the U.S."

I Drew The Short Straw

Our U.S. team of volunteers was still functioning faithfully, but it had become a much bigger job than they signed up for. Jana and I both sensed that as much as we hated to say goodbye to our home, our friends, and our ministry in Central America, we needed to return to North America.

I felt like I'd drawn the short straw. I had to leave the front line, hands-on, fun stuff behind. By going back to the states to serve these other missionaries, I was multiplying my effectiveness a hundred times, but it was another case of, "OK, Lord, I'll do it, but I don't want to."

When Trinity World Outreach–our now-dead church plant in Kerrville, Texas–closed its doors, we kept its post office box active since we occasionally received personal mail there. When we started T.E.A.M. Missions, we just naturally used the same post office box for the new mission.

Since T.E.A.M. Missions was already functioning with volunteers in Kerrville, that seemed to be the most natural place for us to establish a U.S. base for the growing ministry. But the move presented several huge challenges.

We had donors who supported our ministry to the Guatemalan people. But would they continue to stand with us if our address was in the beautiful Hill Country of Texas? Would they continue to see us as a valid place to invest mission dollars if our ministry was now enabling the ministry of many others, rather than doing the ministry ourselves? Living in the U.S. would mean our expenses were about to skyrocket, and it looked like our income could crash dive.

Why Pastoral Care is a Priority

In addition to the increased costs of living in the U.S., I had also made an expensive commitment to regularly visit each of our missionaries to check on their spiritual health. Going is a good start, but it's not enough. I wanted to make sure they could also stay deployed and stay spiritually healthy while serving.

I'd seen missionary families who were struggling with no one even aware of their plight. Their newsletters focused only on the wonderful things happening in spite of their pain. Their reports to their mission agency, if they had one, only told about how they were spending their time and their money. If the reports were filed promptly and the numbers were good, then it was assumed everything was fine.

But no one was aware their kids were in rebellion, the wife was suffering from depression, and the husband was overworked and about to burn out. And who could the missionary confide in? If he openly revealed his struggles to his mission agency, they might offer help, but they might also just pull him off the field and replace him with someone more mentally and spiritually healthy.

Some agencies, like some churches, treat people more like cogs in the machinery than as the treasure for which Christ suffered and died. When a gear in the machine wears out, you simply pull that gear and replace it with another.

Could the missionary confide in his home church and pastor? The pastor might reach out with understanding, but the pastor's primary focus needed to be the sheep at home–the congregation God had given him to watch over. How is he going to find time to understand and invest in a family 8,000 miles away? The most logical response from the home pastor would be, "Come home."

"Come home where we can care for you," sounds like a compassionate option. But "home" for the missionary is now his host country. And moving back to the U.S. or Canada is actually moving *away from home* and adds tremendous stress to an already fragile missionary family.

"Come home" means leaving friends and co-workers. It means returning as discouraged failures. They might be strangers in their home church because many churches experience a 30-80% turnover–depending on how long the missionary has been away. They and their children would have to find new friends, build new relationships, perhaps find new jobs, and adjust to new schools. On top of all that, they would face the very real experience of reverse culture shock. Coming "home" could be the final torpedo that sinks the missionary family's fragile ship.

Consequently, many missionaries find themselves serving and suffering in silence. Who can they open up to without fear of judgment? Who understands the unique stresses of living in another country and culture? Who can appreciate the fact that their home is now another country and that coming "home" to their passport country might actually be the worst thing for them?

I didn't want to, and couldn't, replace the home church pastor, but I saw the need to work with the church, offering the unique understanding and pastoral insights that came with having missions experience myself. And I saw the need to be able to offer pastoral care for those who might not come from a nurturing home church.

To provide this care, I knew I would have to go to where the missionaries were serving – to be on-site with insight. There are some things you can't "see" unless you get face-to-face in their world.

It was easy enough for Jana and me to provide this pastoral care when most of our missionaries were a day's drive away in other parts of Guatemala. Even our missionaries in other countries weren't a problem. I could fly to many countries more cheaply from Guatemala than from the United States.

But now that we had returned to the U.S., and now that I had assumed all the duties that our team of volunteers had been doing, I found myself spending most of my time collecting and depositing money, writing checks, receipting, and keeping books.

I realized I needed to free myself from the bookkeeping duties so I could look after the true treasure of the mission–its people.

NEVER SAY "NO" FOR SOMEONE ELSE

As I thought and prayed about who could help with the bookkeeping, one person kept coming to mind —Joyce. She and her husband, Buddy, had been faithful members of Trinity World Outreach Church–our now-failed church plant. Like my family, they had sacrificed a lot and given of themselves to keep Trinity World Outreach afloat. They believed in us, and they believed in missions.

But there were many reasons I hesitated to ask her. It had been around five years since I'd talked with them. That made it awkward to come asking for a favor. Plus, I didn't even know if she had any bookkeeping or computer experience, or if she would be willing to learn.

But the biggest reason she didn't seem like a logical fit had to do with their adult son. Almost ten years earlier, he had been paralyzed in a tragic accident and was now in a nursing care facility in a nearby town. Every day Joyce traveled 30 minutes each way to sit with her son to make sure he was well cared for all day. If she helped me, she would be giving up time with her son and possibly sacrificing the care he would receive. There was no way she would say "yes."

But her name kept coming to mind when I prayed about a book-keeper. I realized I had no right to say "no" for her. To fail to even ask was to risk robbing her of an opportunity to give... robbing her of an opportunity to receive... robbing her of an opportunity to joy-ously serve. I had to ask her. However, I also knew I wouldn't get a quick answer. Joyce and Buddy didn't do anything without first pray-ing about it.

"Joyce, will you pray about being our first T.E.A.M. Missions bookkeeper?"

"I'll do it," she said.

"Ok, well let me know when you have an answer."

"No, I mean I'll be your bookkeeper."

While I was happy to have such a quick answer, I was also con-fused. "Don't you want to pray about it?"

Her response was rather stunning. "No, I don't need to pray about it. Six years ago when you moved to Guatemala, the Lord told me you were going to come back to Kerrville and that when you did I was going to be helping you. I have just been waiting for you to ask. So, if you need a bookkeeper I'll be your bookkeeper."

Joyce served with us for three years and when we acquired our own offices, her husband, Buddy, stepped in to care for the mainte-nance and upkeep of our building.

No One Accomplishes God's Purpose Alone

I was beginning to see another major principle in God working through ordinary people. No one accomplishes God's purpose alone. You're going to need other people. You're going to need help.

Asking for help is hard. It shouldn't be. If God is doing something wonderful and I'm excited to be part of it, why wouldn't I want to invite my friends to join me? But we fear rejection. We fear appearing foolish, inadequate, weak, dependent. And it seems like missionaries are always asking for something.

Will you pray for us?

Will you support us financially?

Can you help us find a vehicle and a place for our family of five to stay while home on furlough?

Can you help me file this paperwork with the government?

On one trip back to the U.S., I even had to ask for help using the new self-service, swipe your own credit card, gas pump. I felt like a total imbecile staring at this pump with no idea how to get it to give me some gas. I thought about asking with a fake accent so everyone would think I was a foreigner. It was very humbling.

Not only that, but our asking feels harder because usually there's no way we can return the favor. A friend takes our family of five to the airport at 4:30 a.m. They park and help us drag a thousand pounds of luggage to the check-in. We hug and wave goodbye at security. Then we're off and out of their life for years. We won't be around in a month when they need help moving. We won't be there to help when they're sick or lose a job. All we can do is say a deeply sincere "Thank you," and fly away.

It's even harder to ask for financial help or explain why we need to raise support. One shocked fellow summed it up, "You mean to tell me that mission agency asks you to come work for them, but then they don't pay you? In fact, you have to pay them so you can work there?!"

"Yeah, it's crazy isn't it?"

We begin to wonder if people dread seeing us coming, afraid we're going to ask for something. Surely folks are tired of us asking because we sure are. Sometimes we feel like leeches. On the field we give, give, and give some more, but whenever we're home, with family and friends, it seems like we always have our hand out needing something.

WHEN A MISSIONARY IS ASKING FOR HELP HE IS SAYING...

I've discovered that when a missionary is asking for help, he's saying some important things.

A missionary who's asking is saying, "God has given me a vision bigger than I can accomplish on my own."

A missionary who's asking is saying, "You can be part of this great adventure and share in the joy and excitement."

A missionary who's asking is saying, "By sharing with me in the planting, you will also get to share with me in the reward of the harvest."

A missionary who's asking is saying, "There are bigger mountains to climb and wider rivers to cross. The job is huge, but together we can get it done."

A missionary who's asking is inviting others to join him in laying up treasure in heaven by investing in blessing the nations.

It's when a missionary stops asking that we need to be concerned. Have they listened to false accusations, given up, or given in to discouragement? To avoid the humility required to ask, have they decided to pare down the Lord's dream and settle for what they can do in their own strength and with their own resources?

If one of the most powerful men of the Old Testament, Moses, needed Aaron and Hur to hold up his arms so another spiritual giant, Joshua, could win the battle, then surely the battle we're engaged in will require others to stand with us and help us lift the load.

YOUR TEAM IS WAITING FOR YOU TO ASK

And here's the most wonderful news: If you're a Moses, God has already provided your Aaron and Hur. If you're an Aaron or Hur, your participation in the battle means you get to share equally in the victory prize.

Moses, your prayer team is out there. Your financial support team is out there. Your co-workers are out there. The people you'll need are waiting for you to find them and ask them. This is God's dream. Like David gathering the material so Solomon could build the temple, God has already assembled all the people and resources you'll need to accomplish His dream for you. You just need to find them. They are waiting for you to ask. Never say, "No" for someone else.

Aaron and Hur, when you invest in a missionary, you become an essential partner. The battle cannot be won without the strength you add. And you can be sure you will share in the spoils of victory as God fulfills the dream. If doing something as simple as giving a cup of cold water guarantees you'll be rewarded, imagine how great the reward will be if you're regularly investing sacrificially as part of a missionary's home support team.[40]

Years before I had a need, the Lord prepared Joyce to help. He has people already assigned to help you as well. This eases the burden on you, but it also fulfills the dream He has put in their heart. It's a win-win-win. But you need to be courageous and humble enough to ask, and then graciously let others share in the joy of using their gifts and resources to advance God's kingdom dream.

Joyce was the first of the amazing folks God was going to send to enable T.E.A.M. Missions to "help ordinary people partner with God," but she certainly would not be the last. I didn't know it at the time, but God had a whole line of incredibly talented people He was getting ready to send our way.

If you want to go fast, go alone. If you
want to go far, go together.

- AFRICAN PROVERB

■ ■ ■

God's pre-vision leads to His provision.

- RICK MALM

■ ■ ■

I will answer them before they even call to me.
While they are still talking about their needs,
I will go ahead and answer their prayers!

- ISAIAH 65:24 NLT

■ ■ ■

Your Father knows exactly what you
need even before you ask Him!

- MATTHEW 6:8 NLT

CHAPTER 8

You're Full-Grown Adults

■   ■   ■

WHEN ELLIS AND BETTY JOINED TEAM Missions, it immediately became the fastest growing mission agency in the world. Overnight we doubled in size–from one couple to two!

They were the first installment in God's promise to send a team. He started with the least likely of candidates. And it was people just like them that God was going to assemble over the next several years to allow our tiny organization to have a global impact. However, the impact didn't start globally. It started in the smallest of ways.

Initially Ellis and Betty weren't able to raise enough money to buy a car, so they became known to the local Mayan people as "the missionaries that walk everywhere." Some academic missiologists might praise them for practicing *"incarnational ministry"*–living like the folks they ministered to. Some mission agencies would say they were terribly underfunded and needed to go home and raise more support.

I just said, "You're full-grown adults. You can determine for yourself if you need to go home and raise more money or be content walking and eating rice, beans and tortillas every day. I'll stand with you and help you whichever way you choose to go."

Treating CTEN missionaries like responsible adults has been a core philosophy from the start. They can pray and hear from God. They can make decisions for themselves about budgets, lifestyles, when they leave, where they live, who they're going to serve and how they can most effectively accomplish the Lord's purpose. If a missionary can't hear from God on these basic issues, why in the world would we send them to represent Him among the nations?

I've had seasoned missionaries get joyfully teary eyed when I told them CTEN would treat them like adults who could decide for themselves how to best care for their family and how to most effectively reach their area. Many had suffered from cookie cutter, one-size-fits-all rules that just didn't fit their unique situation or ministry.

Ellis and Betty both seemed content living like their neighbors with no savings, no health insurance, no retirement plans, and surviving on the simplest of meals. I don't recommend this because it can lead to early burnout for a missionary and hardship on the family. So, every time I talked with Ellis, I would encourage him to raise more support. Each time, Ellis would look down at the ground, kick some dirt, and agree that he should. And each time, we both knew he wouldn't.

But that was OK. I had walked with the Lord long enough to learn He never equipped me to be anyone's Holy Spirit. They needed to obey what they understood the Lord was asking them to do. Right or wrong, these servants would give account to their Master—not to me. How much money they needed to raise was something they had to come to terms with on their own.

How Much Money Should a Missionary Raise?

This begs the question, "Doesn't a mission agency have a responsibility to make sure the missionary has adequate funding?" I think it does.

But then the question becomes, "How much is adequate?" I believe the answer is, "Enough to be effective."

In Luke 10, Jesus sent His disciples on a mission. He told them to take nothing with them. I can't imagine giving that advice to one of our missionaries, but Jesus did. Later He asked how that worked out for them.

"When I sent you out without purse or bag or sandals, did you lack anything?" 'Nothing,' they answered."[41]

They took nothing, but they were effective. He then immediately tells them to take all those things with them next time. God deals differently with different people at different times. Each person must discern God's will for them—through His Word, through prayer, and through the guidance of the Holy Spirit. Then obey.

We're effective when we're obedient. Boatloads of money can't make us effective. All the latest technology and gadgets can't make us effective. The best missions strategy can't make us effective. These things aren't bad. In fact, they're all very good unless we think they're the keys to effectiveness and success.

Obedience is the key. Apart from Him, we can do nothing. If God isn't working in the hearts of people, our best efforts, slickest presentations, and best laid plans will only produce useless "wood, hay, or straw".[42] Obedience, not money, produces effectiveness and success in ministry.

One of the most effective missionaries I know was terribly underfunded. My heart went out to him when I read this raw and honest report he sent to a sponsoring church. "I'm hungry and thirsty. My clothes are rags. Now and then I even get beaten by the locals." As bad as it was, he didn't ask the church to send more money, and they didn't tell him to come home because it was too dangerous. Does that sound crazy?

Yet I personally know he was very effective. In another letter he wrote:

"I know what it is to be in need, and I know what it is to have plenty. I have learned the secret of being content in any and every situation, whether well fed or hungry, whether living in plenty or in want. I can do everything through him who gives me strength."[43]

God used Paul's pain to teach "the secret of being content." His lack led to his learning: "I can do everything through Him." I'm convinced God sometimes dries up every other resource so we're forced to focus on Him as our only true source.

Naturally, we want to avoid hardship or lack. We want to eliminate risk. But God wants us to discover the joy of contentment, "whether well-fed or hungry, whether living in plenty or in want."

Paul had to live it to learn it. We do too. The Bible can inform us, but experience transforms us. As we personally experience his peace and provision in the midst of our struggles, trusting Him ceases to be a theory. Slowly and painfully it becomes woven into the fabric of our faith.

I'm not saying we intentionally send underfunded missionaries, take foolish risks, or make it harder than it has to be. I'm saying we need to be people of obedience, even if it doesn't make sense.

How Do We Measure Success?

Sometimes obedience will lead to situations that don't appear to be successful. Was Paul a success sitting in a Roman prison? We agree Peter was a success when the angel delivered him from prison, but was James just as successful when, days earlier, in the same prison, he was martyred?[44] Were the unnamed faithful in Hebrews 11 a success even though they died without receiving what God promised?

We must measure success by obedience—not numbers, miracles, head counts, or any other standard. At CTEN we want to be a mission that helps people be successful by being obedient.

A dream I have for Commission To Every Nation (and I believe it's a dream from the heart of God) is that when the next William Carey[45] or Gladys Aylward[46] hears God say, "Go," they won't have to battle endless barriers to obey. I dream they'll find a team at CTEN that will cheer them on, encourage them, and let them know they can do this–because God is able to make them stand.

The Dangers of Sending the Unqualified

I realize there are many potential problems with sending unqualified people. They could have conflicts with other missionaries, leading to hurt feelings. If they're really immature, their disagreements might get so bad that they split up and go their own way–like Paul and Barnabas.[47]

If not properly prepared, they might waste valuable time and resources with false starts, bouncing from place to place trying to find where they should go and what they should do–like Paul and his missions team.[48]

If they aren't culturally savvy, they could easily offend local customs, perhaps even start a riot–like in Philippi and Ephesus.[49]

If they can't raise their budget, they could end up "hungry and thirsty... or even shivering in the cold, without enough clothing to keep warm."[50]

Yes, it's risky to send unqualified people, but as far as I can tell, there was only one truly qualified missionary ever sent. And right now, He's seated at the right hand of the Father in heaven. Obedience to Him will lead to our success in ministry.

I encourage education and training. I encourage raising abundant resources, financial and otherwise. But above all else, I encourage obedience. When God says, "Go," go. If God says, "Now," go now, regardless of what the bank statement says.

The Hope For the Unqualified

But what if we go, and we get into trouble?

We've got to look to the One who sent us to also rescue us. The same God who said, "Go" said He would be with us and supply our needs. The same Lord who invited Peter to join Him on the water reached out and saved Peter when the wind and waves overwhelmed him.

To be honest, it's scary to treat people like "full grown adults." As much as we encourage, counsel and, yes, probably even nag, there will always be those who don't behave like we think they should. Some won't fully learn the language. Some won't adequately communicate with us or donors. Some won't save for emergencies, retirement, or other predictable needs. Some will take foolish risks thinking it is "faith."

Something inside us wants to assume responsibility for them–to legislate what we consider responsible behavior. It would be easier to treat our missionaries like immature kids and make important life decisions for them. We could make sure they don't do anything risky. We could make sure they're fully funded and are saving for furlough, insurance, retirement, and for any and all possible contingencies. We would lessen our liabilities for any "foolish" choices they may make.

We could make sure they never step out of the boat and nearly drown, that they never attack a huge army with torches and pitchers, that they never offend others and end up in a fiery furnace or lion's den. We could make rules to ensure they never need to see God come through in supernatural ways because they are desperately dependent upon Him. But at what cost?

I'm convinced God's goal in sending missionaries is often more about what He wants to do *in* the missionary than what he wants to do *through* the missionary. Just as God used Paul's missions experience to teach him important lessons about contentment and depending on God's strength, I believe God still uses missions as a refiner's furnace for the missionary.

In fact, is it possible that our service here on Earth is more about God changing us than about us changing the world? It sure seems to work out that way.

Ask any missionary. No matter how big their impact, I guarantee they'll say they received more than they gave. "Give and it shall be given unto you." When we go to bless others, God pours blessing back into our lives, "pressed down, shaken together and running over."[51]

Struggles are an unavoidable part of the believer's life. They are a major tool in learning to hear, trust, and follow the Lord. What appears to be a painful failure may be God working the greatest of victories to honor His name. To the natural eye, the Son of God hanging on a cross was a horrific, tragic failure. From God's perspective, it was the greatest of triumphs.

You Are More Qualified Than You Think

The fact that Ellis and Betty, like 98% of their neighbors, were unable to afford a car, gave them a high level of visibility and credibility in their village. Like their neighbors, they were regularly seen walking the dirt roads, coughing from the clouds of dust that would swallow them as a bus zoomed past (or a brand new white SUV with the big black letters "U.N." on the door).

They shopped where everyone else shopped. They were approachable and, like their neighbors, they lived in constant dependence upon the Lord.

As much as they tried to learn Spanish, they never became totally fluent despite their total immersion. But their simple vocabulary wasn't a big problem because Spanish was also the second–or third, fourth, or fifth–language of most of the people they served. As children, many learned several Mayan languages before attending school for a few years where they were forced to speak their first Spanish.

After Ellis and Betty completed their one-year commitment with the agricultural project, the Lord continued opening astounding doors of ministry. They worked with medical and dental teams, teams from Intervarsity Fellowship, and helped at schools and clinics.

Think about that. Here's a couple with no college experience leading teams of college students. A couple with no medical training that became important members of medical and dental teams. All because they made themselves available. Instead of focusing on what they didn't have, they offered what they did have. The Lord took their inadequate, unqualified loaves and fishes and multiplied them in extraordinary ways.

What has God deposited into your life? He wants to use every skill, talent, and experience, all your education, and even your failures and mistakes to bring honor to Himself and to bless His kingdom. Compared to the overwhelming and endless needs of people around the world, what you have is totally inadequate. But when you place it all—failures, successes, strengths, and weaknesses–in the Lord's hands, He can take it, break it, and infinitely multiply it.

To the natural eye, it looked like Ellis and Betty didn't even have enough for themselves. In spite of that, they often loaned money to the Lord.

"If you help the poor, you are lending to the LORD–and He will repay you!"[52]

Out of their own lack, they often gave to help the poor around them. One month Ellis wrote to let me know how things were going.

"We have helped many medical teams but when they leave, then what? We are left with the aftermath. If the doctors diagnosed someone with cancer, who can they turn to for help? They look at us and ask, 'Now what do I do?' Every day we must make moral decisions asking ourselves, 'How far do we go to help?'

"Many of our neighbors can't read, so arranging for medical tests, getting to Guatemala City (6 hours by bus), and arranging treatment is beyond their frame of reference. One month we used almost our entire month's income to help Feliciana who was diagnosed with tuberculosis. We didn't set out to do that, but as we helped her through the process, one thing led to another, and there was no one to foot the bill except us."

He went on to tell how they needed to get her to Guatemala City for a treatment, but had absolutely no money to do it. They stopped by a friend's house and while there, the friend reminded them of a loan they had given her. The friend repaid the entire amount, and it was enough to get Feliciana in for her next treatment!

There were rough times and times of discouragement. But God miraculously provided for every need as they learned to lean on and listen to Him. Ellis and Betty were making a huge difference and daily demonstrating the amazing things God will do if we will simply put ourselves out there and risk the glorious.

I'm Not Very Smart But...

Then one day, Ellis came to me with a problem.

"So many of the people–even the Christians–live in fear because they don't understand what God has done for them. I want to teach the Bible."

He realized the Bible knowledge he had acquired while attending a good Bible teaching church in the US for many years made him more knowledgeable about Scripture than most of the pastors in the area–none of whom had any formal Bible training and many of whom had no more than a sixth grade education.

"Well, let's pray Ellis, and see what God does."

Some weeks later, I heard from him. He was thrilled as he told me the story. "A few nights ago, I heard a knock at my side door. It was one of the pastors. When I invited him in, he asked me if I would teach him the Bible."

Wow. God was fulfilling the dreams of a simple guy who "wasn't very smart, but could work hard" and blessing a local pastor at the same time. Ellis continued, "I asked him where in the Bible he would like to start studying. I suggested the book of Romans."

"*Whoa!*" I thought. "Romans is filled with some of the deepest theology and most profound thoughts of the entire New Testament. Would Ellis be able to pull this off?"

Ellis was still excitedly telling the story. "I asked him, 'Before we start, do you have any questions about the book of Romans?' The pastor thought for a moment and then asked me, 'Who wrote it?' We've been studying together every day for over a month now."

No matter where you are in your walk with the Lord, there's always someone who knows less than you that you can teach. There's always someone who needs help where you have a skill. There's always someone who can be encouraged by hearing what God's done in your life. And there's always someone who can teach and help you.

God used an ordinary guy–with a willing heart and no magic set of skills–to disciple a pastor who was anxious to learn in a remote village in Guatemala. Ellis had gained their respect. He had earned a hearing. Perhaps due to his being "underfunded," he was approachable enough that this pastor felt comfortable humbling himself and asking Ellis to teach him the Bible.

Talk about impact. Who knows how many lives Ellis and Betty touched because they stepped out to do what God put in front of them. They had a massive impact in the area, and for God's kingdom.

I was humbled and amazed when I saw what God did through them. But in the years since, I've seen it happen again and again with hundreds of other ordinary people. **God uses ordinary people to accomplish the extraordinary.** It's not just a cute slogan for Commission To Every Nation. It's God's heart for His people, and He dramatically illustrated just what He means by it through our first missionary couple.

Years later, as I thought about Ellis, I realized the way he first described himself was actually a pretty good one-line job description for missionaries.

I am not very smart, but I can work hard.

How "smart" are you if you volunteer to leave your home, your family, your culture, to abandon career plans, and everything you're familiar with, to raise your own support and go to another country? How smart are you if you live among people you will probably never fully understand, to bring them a message that often is not welcomed or wanted? It's a job description that sounds dangerous, like a lot of hard work, and certainly not something a smart person would do.

But it sounds just like something God would do since He "chose things the world considers foolish in order to shame those who think they are wise. And He chose things that are powerless to shame those who are powerful. God chose things despised by the world, things counted as nothing at all, and used them to bring to nothing what the world considers important."[53]

"Not called!" did you say?
"Not heard the call," I think you should say.
Put your ear down to the Bible,
and hear Him bid you go.

- WILLIAM BOOTH, FOUNDER OF THE SALVATION ARMY

■ ■ ■

Let me consider the poor, and the Lord will consider
me. Let me look after little children, and the Lord
will treat me as His child. Let me feed His flock,
and He will feed me. Let me water His garden,
and He will make a watered garden of my soul.

I may care about myself until I grow morbid; I may
watch over my own feelings till I feel nothing; and
I may lament my own weakness until I grow almost
too weak to lament. It will be far more profitable for
me to become unselfish and out of love to my Lord
Jesus begin to care for the souls of those around me."

- A.B. SIMPSON, FOUNDER OF THE CHRISTIAN
AND MISSIONARY ALLIANCE

CHAPTER 9

What Openings Do You Have In Missions?

■ ■ ■

As WE CONTINUED TO GROW, it soon became evident that Jana and I needed someone to help us care for the missionaries–someone who could help administer the day-to-day activities as well as share the joy and responsibility of visiting the missionaries on the field.

Of course, it wouldn't be easy to find such a person. T.E.A.M. Missions was not a famous mission agency with contacts around the world. Very few people even knew we existed. This proposed new Associate Director would need to move to Kerrville: a nice place, but not on many people's bucket lists of places to live before they die.

The one thing we did have going for us was an unlimited salary package. We could pay as much as they could raise. That's right. We felt the Associate Director should raise his or her own support, just like we did and like we expected of the missionaries.

Because we really didn't know what we were looking for and because we weren't offering a salary, we didn't have a clue how to find someone for the job–so Jana and I prayed and waited. We didn't know it, but that would become our hiring model for future staff, too–prayer and patience.

One day I received an unsigned, one-line email. It looked like spam that had been eBlasted to a huge list. "What openings do you have in missions?" I didn't know where it was from, who was asking, what they wanted, or how they got my email address. It would have been easy to hit delete and move on. But I felt it was basic courtesy to at least give a polite response.

I wrote back explaining that we didn't have "openings," but that I would be happy to talk with them and see if we could connect them with a place to serve. I figured that would be the end of it, but surprisingly, the man emailed back that he was going to be in Kerrville in two weeks and would like to stop in and talk with me about it.

He was from Washington, D.C. but was going to be in Kerrville in two weeks? How random is that? And his wife would be with him so we could meet her, too? It all seemed just odd enough that possibly God was in the mix. But Jana and I agreed not to jump to any conclusions and to take it slowly.

Taking it Slowly

In December 1997, we met Scott and Debra Walston for lunch at a local Mexican food restaurant. Scott was finishing a military career stationed in Washington, D.C. Debra and their seven children were fixing up their dream home in the Amish country of Kentucky–a beautiful farm complete with a stream, expansive meadow, and a large grass-covered hill they lovingly referred to as Walston's mountain.

Being in Amish country, the farmhouse they bought didn't have electricity. Scott told us that Debra wasn't an electrician, but that she wired the entire two-story home. I jokingly asked if she just bought a book and read how to do it. In a very matter of fact way, as though everyone does this sort of thing, she told me that's exactly what she did.

Jana and I could tell these were exceptional people, but at the same time, they weren't superstars. They were ordinary folks–easy to get along with, solid in their faith and convictions: people who just wanted to offer what they had to the Lord. They sure looked like they would be a wonderful answer to our prayer for an Associate Director.

I wanted desperately to ask them about it, but they had expressed interest in mission opportunities. I assumed they wouldn't be interested in a stateside administrative position. Over chips and salsa, I began to tell them about some of our missionaries and how they could come alongside and help them in their ministries.

They politely listened to each opportunity and asked appropriate questions. I couldn't tell if they were totally uninterested in any of the opportunities or if they were just playing their cards close to their chest. By the time the fajitas and enchiladas were history, I had presented every mission opportunity I knew of. Nothing seemed to light a fire under them.

Though I thought they were interested in overseas ministry, I decided I would at least let them know about the Associate Director position. It was administrative "paper-pushing"–nothing as exciting as feeding hungry kids, sharing the gospel on the streets, or learning a new language and culture–but it was the only opportunity we had not discussed.

For the first time, a light came on in Scott's eyes. "Tell me more about that."

I shared all the details of the rather mundane day-to-day stuff I did to help the missionaries so they could do all the fun and exciting things they got to do. I explained that they would have to move from their dream farm in Kentucky to Kerrville. I explained that the salary was nonexistent–that they would have to raise their own support, just like all the missionaries. Nothing seemed to discourage them.

Administration was easy for Scott. That's what he did in the military. He enjoyed it and was good at it. Amazingly, they were willing to sell their dream farm and move to Kerrville. His mother lived in a town about 45 minutes away, and that's why they were in Kerrville now. They already knew that most missionary positions would require they raise their own support, so that wasn't a surprise. Additionally, they had a military retirement that would give them a head start. They were ready and excited about joining the team of T.E.A.M. Missions.

After a long lunch of wonderful Tex-Mex food, Jana and I walked out of Mamacita's Restaurant in a semi-daze. Did I just invite Scott to be our first Associate Director? I think I did.

Did they just say they would sell their dream home and move to Kerrville? I think they did. So much for taking it slowly.

We didn't even know these folks–no references, no background check, no "Let's pray about this," or even think about it overnight.

When decisions like this go well, people praise you as a decisive and insightful leader who's not afraid to take bold steps of action. I wish I could claim that's what happened, but now you know better. I was surprised at what happened and could only hope it was all going to work out for the best.

And it did. Scott finished his military service and like a special confirmation gift from the Lord for taking such a bold step, they were able to sell their farm for twice what they bought it for just three years earlier. This paid for the move and enabled them to buy a home in Kerrville. It's amazing what God does when we take the risk and follow His lead, even when it doesn't make sense.

USE ALL THE BRAINS YOU CAN BORROW

For over ten years, Scott and Debra helped T.E.A.M. Missions navigate some constantly changing waters–a name change, phenomenal growth, an expanding budget, and a technology transformation.

Scott was a visionary who was constantly stretching me and causing me to think bigger. He was willing to take chances and try new things. Some didn't work out, but most were amazing successes that added a lot to our overall ministry as a mission. He thought of things that would have never occurred to me. He looked ahead and established plans and systems that allowed the mission to smoothly expand with minimal growing pains.

He was also a connector of people and had an amazing ability to talk with someone and see twenty places they could use their skills to bless the kingdom. He was definitely God's man for the moment. And Scott confirmed an important lesson about the Lord's method for using ordinary people to do amazing things. To make up for our deficiencies, He will send people alongside to help.

Once He sends these folks our way, we have to overcome our own insecurities, include them in the vision, and help them shine. As President Woodrow Wilson put it, "I not only use all the brains that I have, but all I can borrow." When we use all the brains we have and all we can borrow, our dream is propelled forward, and others also find a fulfilling place of ministry.

That's one of the most beautiful things about how God uses ordinary people. God doesn't bless in a vacuum. Our obedience has a ripple effect sending out blessing and fulfillment into the lives of others as well.

Many times my eyes have filled with tears during one of our orientations as I look out over a room filled with excited missionaries, many preparing to go for the first time and many only able to go because Commission To Every Nation believed in them. Tears of joy and awe have run down my cheeks as I've realized that my simple act of obedience is enabling others to fulfill the dream God has for them—to go, to serve, and to bless the nations.

It would have been easy for me to disobey God when He called me to start CTEN all those years ago. I didn't want to leave Missionary Ventures. I didn't see a need for another mom and pop agency. I didn't want to start something new.

And here's the most dangerous part—I wasn't doing anything wrong. In fact, what I was doing was virtuous and effective. I was a missionary serving with an outstanding organization.

But good can become the enemy of God's best. Often obedience requires letting go of something good to reach out for the unknown. Before leaving Missionary Ventures, I couldn't see the end result of my obedience. I could only see what I was giving up. I could only see what I was letting go of.

The Tarzan Principle of Obedience

A principle I've seen is this: until we let go of the good, the best remains just outside our grasp. Perhaps it's a little off beat, but I see this illustrated in the familiar image of Tarzan swinging from vine to vine through the jungle. In order to move forward, he must release one vine and grab the next one that will propel him forward.

If he refuses to release the current vine, he immediately loses all forward momentum and is left hanging awkwardly in the trees. In the same way, to follow God, we often must let go of what has served us well and taken us this far. To go forward, we must release the good and grab the next vine.

I've known several people who seemed stuck in their spiritual walk–like Tarzan dangling in the treetops. Often they were busy doing good things, just not fulfilled. At one point in their life they chose to cling to what was safe, rather than grasp a vine of uncertain opportunity.

Will that next vine support my weight? Is it secure? Where will it take me? They prayed, but received no promises from God other than, "I will be with you." Fear kept them grasping the safe vine, and at that moment their forward momentum stopped.

There's no way we can know ahead of time if that vine is secure. We can't know if it will hold us, or drop us to the jungle floor. But we can be sure that to continue moving forward, we must let go of what is secure and, trusting God's care and guidance, grab the next vine of obedience. When we do, not only do we surge forward, but the jungle around us comes alive. Branches bend, leaves rustle, monkeys chatter, and birds flap and squawk. Our obedience impacts others and sets in motion amazing and unpredictable spiritual forces.

I couldn't understand that God telling me to start a mission agency wasn't about me. It was about God fulfilling His promise to His friend Abraham. It was about God fulfilling the dreams He would deposit into the hearts of thousands of others. It was about sending them out to bless millions around the world.

This is God's MO–modus operandi. And it's the way He wants to operate in your life, too.

Obedience Starts a Tsunami of Blessing

Like a pebble dropped in a quiet lake, an act of obedience sends out ripples that, instead of getting smaller, actually build to produce tsunami waves of blessing that reverberate for generations. Your choice to obey–or disobey–will produce incalculable results. Obedience sets in motion a generational avalanche of blessing for us, our children, our children's children, and countless others.

"He is a faithful God who keeps his covenant for a thousand generations and lavishes His unfailing love on those who love Him and obey His commands."[54]

Right now, you might be struggling to obey God. Obedience can be scary. Obedience can seem illogical. Obedience can be misunderstood by others. Obedience can be costly and require sacrifice.

But the cost of disobedience is far greater. We have no way to measure what we sacrifice, what we miss out on, and what loss we suffer when we disobey. We never know what might have been, what God might have done, how far the effects of our obedience could have reverberated, and how many lives could have been impacted if we had simply trusted and said, "Yes, Lord."

> For all sad words of tongue and pen,
> The saddest are these,
> "It might have been."

– JOHN GREENLEAF WHITTIER

Our First Offices

Scott was our first full-time staff member, but we didn't even have a place to put him. When Joyce started as our bookkeeper, we knew we had to move our impressive international office out of the large closet in our bedroom. We attended Grace Bible Chapel where the pastor had frequently mentioned that I should let him know if they could ever help with anything. Here was their chance. I asked.

Not only did they freely offer an office that Joyce and I could share, but they threw in a bonus. "Feel free to use our copiers, fax, phones, internet, office equipment, and supplies at no cost."

Wow! What an amazing blessing, because all we had at the time was one outdated computer, a couple of reams of paper, and a few pens with the names of hotels on them. This was an astounding gift.

"But," Pastor Keith went on, "we have been looking for an administrator for our school. Is there any way you could help us out in that area?"

For two years, in exchange for office space, I led Grace Christian School as well as oversaw the expanding mission. It made for a busy schedule, but it allowed us to keep our overhead to near-zero and focus on helping the growing number of T.E.A.M. Missionaries. When Scott joined our staff, the church graciously allowed us to expand into a second office.

It wasn't long, however, until we realized we needed even more space. I just couldn't bring myself to ask the church for a third office. But if we moved, that would also mean we needed to purchase thousands of dollars worth of office equipment, plus incur monthly rent, utilities, maintenance and other overhead.

T.E.A.M. Missions Meets T.E.A.M.

Additionally, we faced another big expense–legal fees. Thanks to this new thing called the internet, I had learned about The Evangelical Alliance Mission and was a little concerned about folks confusing us— T.E.A.M. Missions–with them: T.E.A.M. But I dismissed the concern.

They were a huge organization near Chicago, and we were just three folks in borrowed offices in a small town in Texas. Hardly anybody even knew we existed. Plus, we were tiny little T.E.A.M. Missions. They were The (huge) Evangelical Alliance Mission that had been around over 100 years. Who could confuse us?

Then I received a letter from Illinois and T.E.A.M. They politely asked us to change our name to avoid any possible confusion. I was impressed with the courteous and godly approach they took. No threats, no warnings. Just a suggestion, which added that they were concerned that some donations intended for us might accidentally be sent their way.

I jokingly told Scott that swapping donations with T.E.A.M. sounded OK with me. "Most of their donations are probably bigger than ours. We'll just keep theirs, let them keep ours, and we'll call it even."

Though I joked about it, I realized it was something I needed to seriously consider. "Lord, is it a wise use of Your funds to change our name? It'll cost hundreds of dollars–dollars given by hardworking people to advance the cause of missions. It will affect all of our missionaries–dozens of people–and their donors. Should I 'waste' mission money on the far out chance that tiny T.E.A.M. Missions in Texas will be confused with The (mega) Evangelical Alliance Mission in Illinois? We want to do what's right. Let us know if we should change our name."

I love–in fact I depend upon–the fact that God knows how to communicate clearly, even to those of us who are slow to hear. "He remembers that we are dust."[55] I'm just a pile of dirt with His living breath in me. And I don't know much about following Him, but He knows everything about leading me.

Within weeks, one of our missionaries called. "A donor says he sent a large gift and hasn't received a receipt. He's asking if we got the funds." We contacted the donor to see what happened. "Oh yes," he assured us, "I sent it a month ago to your Illinois office."

Oops. We didn't have an Illinois office, but we knew someone who did. We contacted The Evangelical Alliance Mission. They had been holding the check because they didn't know who it was for. They forwarded it to us. The missionary got his money, and we got our answer. We were going to have to bite the bullet and make the change. But it would be costly, and we didn't have any extra. We needed more office space, thousands of dollars worth of office equipment, and now money for legal fees and research to make sure we wouldn't have to change our name again in the future.

My experience with debt at Trinity World Outreach had confirmed the truth of Proverbs–"the borrower is slave to the lender."[56] I believe God's lack of provision is as directional as His provision. If the funds were not there, God was either saying, "Don't do it," "Do it another way," "Do without," or "Wait."

If God wanted us to move, purchase office equipment, and change our name, He would have to provide the funds ahead of time. I wasn't going to look to a bank for the funds and then look to God to make the monthly payments. We needed a big financial miracle.

I didn't know it, but one of the biggest miracles yet was about to happen.

The essence of surrender is getting out of
God's way so that He can do in us what
He also wants to do through us.

- A.W. TOZER, AMERICAN PASTOR AND AUTHOR

■ ■ ■

But we never can prove the delights of His love
Until all on the altar we lay;
For the favor He shows, for the joy He bestows,
Are for them who will trust and obey.

Trust and obey, for there's no other way
To be happy in Jesus, but to trust and obey.

- JOHN H. SAMMIS, AMERICAN MINISTER,
HYMNIST AND BIBLE TEACHER

CHAPTER 10

Now I Know Why God Wanted
Me To Come On This Trip.

■ ■ ■

AFTER CHURCH ONE SUNDAY, A fellow approached me. "Hi! My name is Tony, and I feel like I'm supposed to go with you on that mission trip." We were taking a team back to Guatemala and had invited folks in the church to go with us. "My wife is due to have our fifth child right around the time of the trip, so it isn't a good time, but I think I'm supposed to go."

I encouraged him to pray about it some more and ask the Lord to confirm His will one way or another. The next week, Tony excitedly let me know he would be going with us. As crazy as it sounds, his wife also felt he should go, so he was in. Several weeks later, he kissed his wife and children, including his one-week-old newborn daughter, goodbye. We boarded a plane and were off.

As we visited various missionaries and ministries, I could see Tony's heart was touched deeply by the overwhelming needs of the people. As we toured an orphanage, Tony pulled me aside. "Now I know why God wanted me to come on this trip."

He told me a remarkable story. A number of years ago one of Tony's clients, who was also a good friend, made an unusual request. Upon the client's death, he wanted Tony (who was his estate planning attorney) to distribute his large estate to charitable causes of Tony's choosing. During the time between when Tony committed to go on the trip and the date of the trip, this friend (and client) passed away, leaving Tony with a very large estate to distribute. He wanted to meet many of the needs we saw on this mission trip, and he also wanted to distribute a million dollars to T.E.A.M. Missions! Really?!!

When to Break Into Your Happy Dance

Was God going to do this? Would there really be a large gift coming our way? It would be nice, but I wasn't going to count on it. I wasn't even going to pray for it.

I believe in prayer. I believe God can do anything. I not only believe in, but I regularly depend upon miracles from His hand.

But I'd been in missions long enough to see a lot of promises fail to materialize. I'd learned to not break into my happy dance until the check cleared. (I once had a desperately needed $25,000 gift come in. We danced, rejoiced, and deposited the check, only to have it bounce all over the country.)

It's not that people don't have good intentions. It's just that on a mission trip, it's easy to be touched very deeply and make magnanimous promises. Once people return to the "real world," the emotions of the trip can quickly fade, and often their promises and commitments fade, too.

When people let you down or fail to follow through, it can be discouraging. But I've learned that even discouragement is a part of God's plan.

How to Survive Discouragement

Discouragement is part of the normal Christian experience. Elijah suffered discouragement. David suffered discouragement. Jeremiah and other Old Testament prophets had intense times of discouragement.

Contrary to popular Christian folklore, God *will* give you more than you can handle. Jesus was overwhelmed to the point of death.[57] Paul experienced more than he could endure and explained why God allows it.

"(In Asia) We were crushed and overwhelmed *beyond our ability to endure*, [...] But as a result, we stopped relying on ourselves and learned to rely only on God [...]."[58]

It was so important that Paul learn "to rely only on God" that the Lord "crushed" him with more than he could handle. God loves you and me enough to do the same thing for us. He wants to break our self-confidence so we learn "to rely only on God." He wants to deliver us from the snare of looking to some person, some grant, some foundation or special gift as our source. He wants our dependence to remain completely and totally in Him.

We win when we let discouragement drive us to God, learn to trust completely in His sovereign timing and plan, and keep our hearts free from bitterness, cynicism, or resentment.

If God wanted to bless his ministry—T.E.A.M. Missions–with a million dollar gift, I would welcome it and handle it responsibly, but in the meantime I would just continue to be grateful for His daily provision.

Amazingly, some months later, the check came. Equally amazingly, the check cleared. I was totally unprepared. Now what?

SIT BACK, LISTEN AND LEARN

I prayed and felt the Lord put the names of several local Christian businessmen on my heart. I knew each of these men, and contacted them to ask them to pray with me and advise me on how to wisely invest the funds and locate office space.

We didn't need anything fancy. I envisioned buying a small piece of land outside of town and dragging a mobile home onto it. Voila! Our new offices!

When I made this suggestion, the looks on their faces told me I needed to just sit back, listen, and learn.

As they discussed the options, I learned a lot. Once again, I learned the wisdom of humility, the wisdom of not only using all the brains you have, but all you can borrow. They considered it from every perspective—build, buy, lease, in town, out of town, prime property, or the backside of a warehouse.

It wasn't until I listened to each of them putting in their unique perspective that I realized why God had put these men on my heart. Each came with his own area of expertise. They considered all the angles, and together they decided and convinced me we needed to be located in town, and we should look for an office building we could buy.

Buy an office building? How do you even go about doing that? Could we afford a building in town? Aren't those like a brazilian dollars? I had no idea. I'm a missionary who barely passed Algebra. Here I was again, way over my head.

But here I was again, also, opening the door for people to use the talents and skills God gave them to bless His kingdom. We helped missionaries do that. Now I was seeing that my weakness was also providing an opportunity for these businessmen to experience the same joy–the joy of God using them and their expertise to advance His kingdom.

Faithfully Serving: The First Qualification For Leadership

That's a principle I've seen at work again and again. I believe it's one reason God loves to use inadequate people. The weakness of Moses provided an opportunity for Aaron and Hur to stand beside him and help lift the weight. They helped Moses, which enabled the man on the front lines, Joshua, to win the war. Each had his part in the battle, and each shared in the joy of victory.[59]

During a desperate draught, the needs of Elijah were met by the widow of Zarephath, and in turn, her needs were provided for.[60] God delights to use the weak, the inadequate, and the unqualified. It brings honor to Him and spreads the joy around among His people.

Sometimes you may be the point man of what God is doing, and He will send others to support and help you. Sometimes, you will be the "Aaron and Hur" sent to support others. No matter what your assignment, it's important to do it faithfully.

I've known some who were so anxious to be the point man that they refused to help others when they had the chance. They wouldn't touch the menial tasks because they were waiting to be called to lead the pack. But it's important to serve where you are, doing what you can, no matter how insignificant the task seems.

David was watching sheep when he was called to be king. Elisha was plowing a field when he was called. Matthew was busy collecting taxes. James and John were helping their father in the family business. Peter and Andrew were fishing. Whenever God chooses a person for a big job, He always chooses one who is busy being faithful at a small one.

To be chosen as the lead guy for a God-dream, you need to first be faithful serving behind the scenes, helping fulfill the dreams of others. Jesus put it this way: If you won't be faithful in helping another, "Who will give you your own?"[61]

Be faithful wherever your assignment might be right now. I guarantee, Someone notices.

If it Sounds Too Good to be True...

"What about that building on Jefferson Street?" one of the fellows asked. I knew the one he meant, and it was one of the nicest buildings in town. It was two stories and had a prime location. But it was much bigger than anything we would ever need.

"Is it even for sale?" I asked.

The fellow who made the recommendation said, "I know the guy who owns it. I'll talk to him."

We met a few weeks later and were told the owner of the building was looking at downsizing his investments so he could retire and would sell the building for $500,000. Was that a good deal, top dollar, or a fair price? I had no idea, but the guys on the team knew just what to do. They began researching it.

One discovered the building had been built a few years earlier for $1.2 million. That was good news and bad news. Why was he selling it for only $500,000? Thinking back to my experiences in Guatemala I immediately thought, "Maybe it's built on a fault line." The guys assured me this was a very good but reasonable price, and reminded me I didn't need to worry about earthquakes in Kerrville.

Another discovered the property was fully leased, so he ran the numbers on the monthly cash flow the property produced. We only needed a couple of small offices, so the other tenants would actually be producing income that could help us keep our overhead extremely low.

As each man shared what he discovered, it all looked too good to be true. Surely there was something we were missing. I prayed and waited, then prayed and waited some more. Finally the frustrated seller asked, "Do you want the building or not?"

I nervously took the deal. In October 1999, we dedicated our new offices with an open house and time of prayer and thanksgiving.

For years, I expected the Environmental Protection Agency to show up at our door and tell us our building was located on a toxic waste dump, or that we would discover some other huge problem. It was just too good to be true.

But it was true. Proceeds from the extra office spaces we rented out helped us keep our overhead low as well as invest hundreds of thousands of dollars into projects and disaster relief that have blessed missionaries and people around the world.

Sixteen years after we purchased the building, the previous owner still has not retired. I was told a few years after the sale that he told someone he always loved that building and wasn't even sure why he sold it, especially for such a bargain price.

God had given us a home. Now we needed furniture. When I saw the cost of even inexpensive office desks and chairs, I about choked. We had the money, but I thought, "Imagine how much good our missionaries could do with that much money! Do we really need desks and chairs?"

Then a call came from a friend in Houston who worked for an oil company. They were remodeling their offices and wondered if we needed some used office furniture. You bet! Dan Schoen, a missionary kid who attended church with us, drove his truck and trailer to Houston and brought back God's latest gift—some beautiful solid wood desks, chairs, filing cabinets, and credenzas.

The large gift also allowed us to purchase needed office equipment. And we were able to honor the request of The Evangelical Alliance Mission to change our name.

T.E.A.M. Becomes C.T.E.N.

The name change required a lot of expensive research by a lawyer to make sure we wouldn't have to change it again in the future. During this research it looked like every name imaginable had already been taken. I even found one called "The No Name Mission." I could empathize with them and realized why so many people just name a ministry after themselves. At least your own name is probably available.

I finally stumbled upon a name that seemed right and wasn't already taken. But here I was again, full circle, back to an enormous name, though this one didn't speak so much of an enormous ministry as an enormous mission given by an enormous God: Commission to Every Nation.

At that time, changing the name seemed like such a huge thing. We had dozens of missionaries who would have to explain the change to their donors. Little could I have guessed the growth God had in store for us. But the Master builder was looking over his blueprint, and now He was laying this final piece of the foundation in place. In February 1999, T.E.A.M. Missions became Commission To Every Nation.

With a new name and new offices, God had established a solid foundation for CTEN. I didn't know it, but he was going to continue to send a steady stream of people our way—people who had a dream God had planted in their hearts. People who needed a team to stand with them to fulfill that dream. Ordinary people empowered by an extraordinary God to go and bless the nations.

But we didn't want to just send people. We wanted to be able to care for them and help them stay spiritually healthy while serving. With the added responsibilities and growth came more and more administrative duties. It was getting harder and harder for our small team to visit the missionaries.

Caring for the missionaries by praying for them daily, communicating with them regularly, and regularly visiting them in their country of service was going to fall through the cracks if we didn't get some help.

The answer came in an unusual way.

You do not need a great faith, but faith in a great God.

- HUDSON TAYLOR, MISSIONARY TO CHINA AND
FOUNDER OF THE CHINA INLAND MISSION

■ ■ ■

God's work done in God's way will
never lack God's supply.

- HUDSON TAYLOR, MISSIONARY TO CHINA AND
FOUNDER OF THE CHINA INLAND MISSION

CHAPTER 11

I Can't Find Anyone To Pray With Me About This

■ ■ ■

THE FIRST TIME I MET Jack Rothenflue, I realized he was a little different. He was a conservative, pastoring a church in a liberal denomination. But that's not what made him stand out. Nor was it his jeans and cowboy boots in a sea of businessmen in their suits and ties.

Jack gave a devotional at a businessmen's lunch that I sponsored in our new office conference room. Every week, I invited a different pastor to give a short talk to a group of businessmen who brought their own brown bag lunch. It turned out to be a win-win-win-win God idea.

The lunch brought both businessmen and local pastors into our building to discover Commission To Every Nation, which had come to be affectionately referred to as CTEN (see-TEN) (Win #1). Each man brought his own lunch so I had almost no physical preparations (Win #2). I knew the pastor would bring his best stuff (which meant a powerful devotional thought), and I didn't have any teaching preparations (Win #3). And on top of all that, one of the guys usually bought me lunch (Win #4). What a deal! Like I said, win-win-win-win.

After the meeting, Jack had some questions about missions. I anticipated the routine questions people ask, and I was ready with my routine answers.

Why send missionaries when there are so many unbelievers at home?

Why send missionaries when national workers can do it cheaper and better?

Why send missionaries to countries already "reached" with the gospel?

Why send missionaries when they destroy native cultures?

In case you're wondering how to answer any of these questions, check Addendum 1 in the back of this book to see the answers I was ready to give Jack.

But he caught me off guard. His questions were insightful. They touched upon real issues in missions. This guy in the jeans and cowboy boots impressed me. I tried to provide meaningful answers, but I was really just bluffing my way through, hoping my surface answers would satisfy his profound questions. It was a relief when he said, "Thanks," popped on his white cowboy hat, and waved goodbye.

Told To Resign But Now What?

It was several months before I saw Jack again. He came to my office and asked if I'd pray with him. I thought his request was odd. He pastored a local church and knew hundreds of Christians in town. We hardly knew each other. Why would he ask *me* to pray with him?

"God told me to resign from my church, so I did. But I don't know what I'm supposed to do next. Everybody says I'm crazy, and most won't even pray with me about it. But I figure you're a missionary. You should know something about faith. Would you pray with me as I try to figure out what God wants me to do?"

That was it—he just wanted someone to pray with him. As we prayed, I sensed Jack would be a good fit with our growing ministry, so after the "Amen," I invited him to consider coming to serve with us.

Totally surprised, he asked, "What would I do?"

Obviously I hadn't thought that far ahead. "I have no idea, but I think you'd be a good fit. Why don't you and your wife pray about it and see if this might be what God has for you." We chatted a few more minutes, and he got up to leave.

As he was in the doorway on his way out, I remembered that I hadn't mentioned our unlimited salary package. "Oh yeah, you have to raise your own support to do this."

He got a puzzled look. "How does that work?"

As I explained it, this fish that was about to jump in the boat seemingly swam away. "Ok, thanks for praying with me. We'll be in touch."

A Divine Download

It was almost two months before I saw Jack again. "Tell me more about this support raising thing." He had invitations from three churches to come be their pastor, but he just couldn't shake the idea of doing "who-knows-what" with CTEN. He was beginning to wonder if this might be the direction God was leading. But raising your own salary to do it? That was a little crazy. He said he would continue to pray about it.

I knew from my accidental election to the school board in Guatemala that "praying about it" can be dangerous, and can lead you down paths you never dreamed of venturing down. I hoped that would happen for Jack, too.

Weeks later, I was in a meeting with our board of directors. The door to the conference room flew open and Jack appeared. "Oh, I'm sorry. I have to talk with you later. God spoke to me." And with that, he was off.

Later, Jack told me God had "downloaded an entire pastoral care plan." Jack wrote as fast as he could while the Lord put idea after idea into his head for how CTEN could take pastoral care from good to excellent. This was God. This was something the Lord wanted Jack to be involved in. He didn't know how he was going to raise his support, but he was ready to launch out and see what God would do.

He joined the staff of CTEN and began raising support. A few folks responded, but certainly not enough to pay the bills. But that was OK because his wife, Carol, found a job. Her income, plus a few withdrawals from their savings, enabled them to get by. But God has a way of messing with our best-laid plans.

Carol enjoyed her job, but as months, then years passed, there was a growing sense that it wasn't where she belonged. She belonged with Jack, with CTEN. But the funds just weren't there. One day while she was feeding the goats, chickens, and donkeys (there was a reason Jack wore those boots), she expressed her frustration, "Lord, it's been three years! When are we going to have enough support so I can serve full time with Jack?"

The Lord's response was not very comforting. As he often does, he answered her question with a question, "How much faith does it take if you wait until you have full support?" She sensed the Lord was challenging them to get fully out of the boat and walk with Him in even deeper waters of trust.

It's funny how often we're waiting for God, only to discover that He has been waiting for us. Often we must take the first step. Once we act, He acts. "Draw close to God and (then) he will draw close to you."[62]

It was scary, but Jack and Carol knew it was better to be poor, hungry, and obedient than well-funded, well-fed, and disobedient. Carol quit her job and joined the CTEN staff full time. The very next month, something totally unexpected happened.

Did their income triple? Did a rich uncle die leaving them a million dollars? Jack and Carol obediently stepped out of the boat, courageously trusting God to provide for them. And, the very next month, three of their donors announced that they were going to have to stop supporting them!

Epic Testimonies Require Epic Tests

His ways are certainly not our ways, are they? In our minds we calculate what God's going to do, how He's going to come through for us. But, instead, things sometimes go from bad to worse. It's easy to feel like the fellow who said, "They told me to cheer up, things could be worse. So, I cheered up and, sure enough, things got worse."

We can't have an epic testimony without an epic test. We can't experience a glorious victory without a grueling battle. It's the struggle to escape the cocoon that strengthens the butterfly and enables it to soar.

We shouldn't be surprised if sometimes our obedience leads to things getting worse. Obedience needs to be its own reward. We don't obey as a tool to get something from God. We do what's right, because it's right to do right, regardless of the consequences.

The fact that you're reading this makes me wonder if the Lord has asked you to do something crazy. Something way beyond your ability. It might seem scary and illogical. You might feel inadequate. It might mean sacrificing your career, financial security, or even your reputation. It might be something that you've tried before and failed.

If you'll follow the Lord's invitation, I can't tell you there won't be terrifying moments–there probably will be. I can't tell you doors will fly open with no effort on your part. I can't even promise that if you step out of the boat you won't sink. Peter did–right after he had one of the most breathtaking adventures any human has ever experienced!

Obedience can be terrifying. But I decided a long time ago that if I'm drowning and God throws me an anchor, I'll grab the anchor. I'd rather go down trusting Him than stay afloat on my own. If God takes us to the bottom, it's better to be there with Him than on the surface without Him.

Our Heavenly Father wants the best for us. When we grasp that truth, we can embrace Him and embrace where He takes us. It may not be our preference. It may not be comfortable. We may not understand it. But "we know that God causes everything to work together for the good of those who love God and are called according to his purpose for them."[63]

Isn't it ironic that passage starts out "we know?" Really? We know…? If I really knew God was working all things together for my good I wouldn't respond with anxiety when problems invade my world. I wouldn't retaliate when mistreated. I wouldn't get frustrated when things don't go my way, because I'd realize no matter what's happening, things *are* going my way. If I believed God causes every detail of my life to work together for my good, I'd walk with such incredible peace and confidence it would be like... well, it would be like I was a new creature.

Jack and Carol, like countless other heroes of the faith, and like all our CTEN missionaries, faced that moment where they had to choose between the safety of the boat and the terror of the storm. It looks different for each of us but that "step out in faith or stay locked in fear" moment is part of the core curriculum for all of the Lord's disciples.

God tailor makes our challenges. He customizes each one to demolish our unique set of fears and idols of security. But I guarantee, if God's going to do extraordinary things through you, He's going to confront those things that you cling to in your effort to stay afloat. He wants you clutching only Him–even if He comes looking like an anchor that's going to take you to the bottom.

GOD AND SATAN HAVE THE SAME GOAL

Jesus wasn't sacrificed to make our lives better. He wants us crucified with Him. That means God and the devil have one goal in common. They both want us dead. The death to our old self that Jesus offers is the entrance to a free and thrilling new life–His life. When I'm dead to myself, the Lord can live his life through me. His life, his work, accomplished through me.

When we catch this concept, we understand why God isn't limited by the tiny box of our skills or abilities. He wants to do out-of-the-box incredible things that only He can do–but do them through you and me. The world still hasn't seen what God will do through the man or woman who gets "self" out of the way and is totally yielded to Him.

But how do you handle those internal and external voices that scream, "You can't do this." "You aren't qualified." "You aren't smart enough, strong enough." "You don't have the academic background, the financial resources, or the experience." "You don't have what it takes to walk on water." How do you handle those voices?

Agree quickly with your adversary. Those voices are absolutely right–you can't walk on water. But if you've heard His invitation, step out. Follow His invitation, and watch in amazement what God does.

Jack and Carol heard the invitation. They stepped into the terror of self-abandoned obedience. They stepped into the joy of seeing God do amazing things through them. Jack developed the pastoral care program far beyond what I had imagined, and created a pattern that would be followed by others who would join CTEN as full time pastoral care couples.

Due in a large part to Jack and Carol's influence, every department of Commission To Every Nation—Administration, Finance, Publications, even Building Oversight–sees missionary care as part of their job description. Printing newsletters, depositing checks, answering phones, changing light bulbs–they are all done for the purpose of serving the frontline missionaries. Jack and Carol had an amazing impact.

Curiously, another Jack and Carol were about to impact Commission To Every Nation in an entirely different way.

O CANADA

Jack and Carol Lavallee are a Canadian couple, and CTEN missionaries. One day they came to Scott with a wild idea. Years earlier, they felt the Lord say they should start a Canadian mission agency. They believed now was the time to do it.

As they talked, it made sense that CTEN would work with them in this dream. Scott said he would present the idea to me and see what I thought.

What they didn't know is that years earlier I felt the Lord say we would open a Canadian office. I just had no idea how it would happen, so I put it on the back burner. In Guatemala, God said He would put together a team to "bless the nations." He was doing that. If He wanted a Canadian office, I was confident He could do that too, at the right time. Was this the time? I started praying and seeking counsel.

Jack and Carol had friends in Canada who could help us navigate the legal challenges. A pastor in Windsor, Ontario, offered to serve on the board as well as give us office space at the church. The church treasurer, a retired technician with Ford Motor Company, volunteered to handle the bookkeeping. CTEN USA started with volunteers. Perhaps CTEN Canada could, too. It looked like God was saying, "Now's the time."

We started the paperwork for a Canadian charity. About nine months later, on September 16, 2005, Canada Revenue put the final stamp of approval on the paperwork and Commission To Every Nation Canada was officially up and running.

Good Problems In Canada

John Hauk, our volunteer bookkeeper, was new to computer book-keeping, but he attacked the huge learning curve. He figured out how to handle all the cumbersome details and today, over a decade later, he's still head of our Canadian finance office.

He's such an inspiration to me. He's retired from his career! He could spend every day camping beside a quiet Canadian lake or put-tering around his garage making birdhouses. But he didn't "re-tire." Instead, he chose to "re-tread." He chose to go from success to significance. He is investing his time and energy in something that literally makes a worldwide impact today and for eternity.

It was exciting to watch CTEN Canada grow. Before long we had ten CTENC families. But growth also presents its challenges. I didn't know Canadian law, and our Canadian office was 1500 miles away.

John was doing an amazing job, but he was a volunteer. Jack and Carol were still committed to their missions ministry in US prisons. If a crisis arose, it wouldn't be fair to ask them to drop everything to handle it. Just like CTEN USA quickly grew too big to be effec-tively handled by volunteers, CTEN Canada had now reached that point.

When CTEN USA needed a full-time director, I left our ministry in Guatemala to assume full time leadership of the ministry in the US. But I wasn't the guy to run our Canadian office, and I didn't know anyone who could. The need for full time leadership became such a concern that I actually considered closing the Canadian office.

I told Jana, "I don't want to close it, but I also don't want to be sending missionaries if I can't guarantee we'll be there for them when they need us. It would be better to not send a family than to send them and not be able to support them once they're on the front lines. We need a full-time director, but I don't even know where to start looking."

Our staff recruiting policy had become "prayer and patience," but I have to admit, I didn't have much faith that God could answer this prayer, and my patience was running thin because of my concern for the missionaries who were counting on us.

Only a handful of people even knew about CTEN Canada. I didn't know how to get the word out about the need. And, like the US staff, the Canadian director would have to raise his or her own support.

No salary. No contacts. No way to get the word out. I didn't see how even God could pull this one off. O Canada, I didn't want to, but if something didn't happen soon I felt the only responsible thing to do was pull the plug.

But apparently God also wanted a mom and pop agency in *The True North* because He provided a director in a wonderful way.

GOD'S NOT FINISHED WITH YOU YET

At one of our three-day orientations, a couple going to Greece got excited about how Commission To Every Nation serves and cares for missionaries.

Her father had been a missionary to Greece, but was stepping down. He felt his time in missions was done. Then he received a call from his daughter.

"Dad, you need to check out Commission To Every Nation. They do missions the way you've always said it should be done."

Skeptical, but willing to look into it, Trevor Eby came to the next orientation in March 2011. His daughter was right. CTEN's vision aligned perfectly with his for how an agency could help missionaries go and stay healthy while serving.

As Trevor and I talked, it became clear this man would be an amazing addition to our team. He had missions experience. He loved missions and missionaries. He had seen the need to care for missionaries after sending them. And he was just a very likable, easy-going kind of guy. But aren't all Canadians like that, eh?

Then I discovered that for the last 17 years he had been the Canadian director for the ministry he formerly served with in Greece. If I had written a point-by-point description of the person, personality, and experience we needed for a director, it wouldn't have been as ideal as Trevor.

It was obvious he was God's man for CTEN Canada. Trevor was an amazing answer to a prayer I hadn't even had enough faith to pray. The final confirmation came when I discovered his wife, like my wife, was named Jana. OK, that wasn't a confirmation, but it was interesting and makes for some fun confusion when we're all together.

The most exciting part? Not only was God enabling CTEN Canada to continue sending and serving Canadian missionaries, but the Lord was allowing Trevor to step into a ministry that fulfilled the dream God put in his heart. Just when he thought he was done with missions, God opened a new door of expanded opportunity. In September, 2011, he became the first director of CTEN Canada.

As the director, Trevor would be sending and caring for missionaries, including his daughter and son-in-law, valuing them as the precious kingdom treasures they are.

CTEN USA and CTEN Canada now had great leadership and a growing team of missionaries. When God first started talking to me about establishing a mission agency, He had said He would send a team. He said that team would help fulfill the promise He made to His friend Abraham: that through Abraham's seed, the Lord Jesus, all nations would be blessed. That was beginning to happen.

Around the world, 24/7, 365 days a year, CTEN missionaries were blessing the nations. In scores of different ways, they were sharing the glorious news of God's offer of salvation through Jesus. Things couldn't have been going better until...

Jesus did not die just to save us but to own us. He came not only to free us from sin but to enslave us to Himself.

– JOHN MACARTHUR, AMERICAN PASTOR, AUTHOR AND CHRISTIAN BROADCASTER

■ ■ ■

To do what's right because it's right, even if you don't feel like it, is not hypocritical, it's virtuous. It's called submission. It's called obedience.

– RICK MALM

CHAPTER 12

Don't You Have To At Least Pray About It?

■ ■ ■

In February, 2011, Scott Walston sensed it was time for him to step down as director of CTEN USA. He had done a remarkable job. Together, we had seen the Lord take CTEN from borrowed offices to its own office building, from a few families to hundreds of missionaries around the globe, from manually balancing a checkbook to a high-tech finance and publications department.

He was also key in establishing the Canadian office. His impact would continue to be felt for years and only eternity will reveal the full ripple effect of his ministry. It was hard to imagine CTEN without Scott, but there was also no question in my mind as to whom the person was that the Lord had prepared to step in and take the mission onward. The problem is, that person wanted nothing to do with it.

Jack Rothenflue frequently told me how much he admired how easily Scott carried the heavy director's load. He also mentioned, regularly, that he would never want the director's job. Jack absolutely loved his pastoral care ministry. However, I felt a strong confidence from the Lord that Jack was to be the next CTEN USA Director, so in obedience to God's urging, I presented the opportunity to him. He responded exactly as I predicted - "No. Not interested. I love what I'm doing now."

"But Jack," I reasoned. "Don't you have to at least pray about it?" (Evil laugh goes here.) "Praying about it" led me to founding CTEN. "Praying about it" kept me from resigning from the school board in Guatemala. "Praying about it" started Jack down this crazy missionary road in the first place. "Praying about it" has led many saints into deserts of desperate dependence—a place God seems to enjoy taking His people. I was trusting "praying about it" would also lead Jack to the CTEN USA Director's chair.

We serve an untamable, unpredictable God. He loves to lead us into places – like the bottom of a pit - where we have nowhere to look but up. I was trusting that when Jack "prayed about it" the Lord would say, "Let's go for a walk on the waves."

I am glad God honors obedience even when we don't want to obey. Jack prayed, heard from the Lord, and even though he felt unqualified and didn't want to do it, he took an even bigger step of trust. In April 2011, he stepped into the director position and has done an outstanding job.

The fact that we continue to receive the highest possible ratings from Charity Navigator and other non-profit watchdog organizations attests to his administrative skills. The peace and harmony of the staff attest to his pastoral leadership skills. His flexibility and sensitivity to the Lord make him a joy to serve with.

I continue to be astounded at the quality of staff the Lord sends our way and the amazing missionaries the Lord allows us to serve. And the story continues.

A Confession

As we wrap this up, I need to confess something. But I'd appreciate it if we could keep this just between me and you. Some years ago, a friend and I were talking about Commission To Every Nation when she made this comment: "You have such a heart for missions. I wish I were as missions-minded as you." As soon as she said that, a strange feeling came over me.

Later, as I tried to figure out why her comment produced such a weird sensation, I had a startling revelation. I'm not really "into" missions. I want to see Jesus established as Lord in the United States as much as in Uganda, in Cambodia as much as in Canada. I get as excited about someone coming to the Lord in St. Paul, Minnesota, as in Sao Paulo, Brazil. People are people and the gospel is the gospel. I don't really care about nationality, color of skin, culture or language. We all need Jesus!

I'm not interested in pondering the three waves of missions or what the next great wave will be. I really don't care to explore "the anthropological implications of incarnational ministry upon evangelistic effectiveness in developing nations." I can barely say it! In fact, I avoid conventions where mission leaders are going to talk strategy and philosophy. I just can't get into all that professional missions stuff.

So, I've often wondered, "What am I doing leading CTEN USA and CTEN Canada?" Lord, shouldn't a leader of a mission agency know all the lingo and be able to pontificate about the future of missions or the viability of short versus long term missions efforts, etc.?" I really don't care about all that.

But I absolutely love the assignment the Lord has given me with Commission To Every Nation. I love working with our staff. I love both getting to know and encouraging the missionaries. I'm thrilled to have the privilege of visiting them and working with them in all the nations and cultures where they serve. They are the finest folks you'll ever meet. They're doing amazing things and I love being part of it all. So why do I love all the missions activities my life is filled with if I'm not "into" missions?

My Real Passion

As I thought about it, I realized what I'm "into" is helping people step into the fullness of what God has for them. I'm "into" seeing folks break free from their comfort cages and risk the glorious. I get excited when I see people step out of the boat and be awe struck by what God does in response to their obedience.

I love to see the spike in spiritual growth and faith that takes place when people place themselves in a position where they are totally dependent upon the Lord. And then I love to see them marvel as He shows himself faithful in the most unusual and astounding ways. That's my passion. Missions is just a wonderful tool for seeing that happen.

So now you know my secret. And here's why I needed to share it with you. If, in my 20s, 30s or even 40s, I had sat down and tried to draft a plan for my life and set 20-year goals with steps to accomplish them, I can assure you that starting a mission agency wouldn't have even been on my radar. And because of that, I would have totally missed God's plan. I had no idea what would bring me the greatest joy. I had no idea what my deepest passions were or how to discover them. But God knew.

And He led me, though I was fussing and complaining most of the way, into doing something that ultimately fulfilled a dream I didn't even know I had. He knew what would bring me the greatest joy (and Him the greatest glory), and He led me step-by-step without letting me know where we were going.

THE PATH TO A FULFILLING LIFE

By now you know that I'm not "Mr. Extremely Talented." I'm not "Mr. Dynamic Leader," or "Mr. Gifted Visionary." I'm just an ordinary guy. But I serve an extraordinary God. And here's the real secret I want to share with you.

Because there is nothing special about me, you can be sure that what God has done in my life, He wants to do in yours, too. No, I'm not talking about starting a mission agency. (Unless He tells you the world needs another mom and pop mission agency.) What He wants to do is fulfill the dreams He has placed in you–dreams that you might not even be aware of right now.

You probably think this or that would bring you great fulfillment–and you may be right. But is it possible that God has a path for you that will lead to even deeper and richer fulfillment than you can imagine? Is it possible He wants to do more in and through you than you can dream of or plan for? Could the Gentle Shepherd be trying to lead you into green pastures that will produce amazing joy for you and bring great glory to Him?

It's quite possible the path He points you toward doesn't look like it will take you there. It's quite possible the path appears to go in the opposite direction of where you're dreaming about.

I loved working with Missionary Ventures. I loved leading short-term mission teams. The last thing I wanted to do was get involved in administration and leading a mission agency. But that was the path the Shepherd pointed me down. So obedience said that was the path I would follow–even if I did it with a sour attitude.

There was no way I could know at the time that this path would also produce opportunities and joy beyond what I could have imagined. If I had written a plan for my life, it would not have been as glorious as the one I have been led into by this wonderful Shepherd.

The Lord knows you better than you know yourself. The Lord knows what will truly bring you fulfillment and what will bring Him the greatest glory. The Lord knows the path that will take you there, and is very committed to leading you into that which is best for you.

I want to encourage you to follow the wisdom the Shepherd shared when He said to "seek first the kingdom of God, and his righteousness."[64] I want to encourage you to break free of your doubts and fears and cast yourself fully upon the Lord Who loves you and wants nothing but the best for you. Follow His invitations. Follow the Good Shepherd even if where He takes you makes absolutely no sense.

God is often slow to do great things
through us because we are slow to allow
Him to do great things in us.

- RICK MALM

■ ■ ■

Only one life, 'twill soon be past,
Only what's done for Christ will last.

- C.T. STUDD, BRITISH PASTOR,
AUTHOR AND MISSIONARY

The Book Of Acts Is Still Being Written

■ ■ ■

STRANGELY, THE BOOK OF ACTS, the story of the early church and early missionaries, starts with a very formal introduction, but there's no formal summary or conclusion to wrap it up. It's like the writer just stops. There's no ending.

Obviously, that's not an oversight. The Holy Spirit orchestrated this to let us know the story continues–perhaps being recorded by heavenly scribes. The Holy Spirit is still at work in our world and in His people. The "acts" continue as we follow His invitations, and He responds in miraculous ways to our obedience. I want to encourage you to be part of God's continuing story.

Today Commission To Every Nation and its hundreds of missionaries are doing what seemed like an impossible dream a few decades ago when God started breaking into my quiet times. Twenty-four hours a day, somewhere in the world, a CTEN missionary is serving, giving, touching lives with the message of God's kingdom. We're part of a great force of missionaries and mission agencies fulfilling the promise to Abraham and blessing the nations.

Your Invitation

As exciting as that is, I hope by now you realize this book isn't just about Commission To Every Nation, or me. It's an invitation. It's your invitation to be part of God's ongoing story. It's your invitation to dream–to imagine what God will do through you when you abandon the ordinary and make yourself fully available to the God of the extraordinary.

If you think that's not for you, let me simply ask, "Don't you have to at least pray about it?" (Friendly smile goes here.)

If you're a new or established CTEN missionary, this book is for you. Now you have a better understanding of the soul of the organization that has joined you in fulfilling the dream God put in your heart. Now you know why everyone at CTEN is so encouraging and so sure you'll be an extraordinary missionary.

We've seen thousands of ordinary people, just like you, timidly step out of the boat to discover they could walk on water. They were able because the Lord Who called them was able–able to make them stand. They experienced the exhilaration reserved for those who leave the safety, security, and familiarity of friends and family to escape their comfort cage and follow the Master's invitation: "Come."

This book is for you if you're finding God intruding in your quiet times and inviting you to join Him in some insane adventure. Perhaps, like I was, you're comfortable where you are and love what you're doing. Why doesn't God choose someone else, someone more qualified, more willing?

Perhaps He's inviting you to join His army of missionaries working with Him to fulfill his promise to Abraham to bless all nations. You may be like Moses. You've already given Him all the reasons He should choose someone else. Did you convince Him? Or did He just tell you what He told Moses: "I'll be with you."

This book is for you if you're one of the tens of thousands of donors who give to CTEN. Now you know the history and heart behind the agency you invest in. Perhaps, as I've shared some of my struggles, you've discovered new ways you can pray for and support your missionary friends, who likely face some of the same insecurities and challenges I do.

Perhaps the Lord is also inviting you to take a bigger step of faith. God doesn't just stretch missionaries. He is just as committed to seeing *your* faith grow–and faith only grows when connected with risk. Can you risk the glorious and invest more in the harvest of the nations?

Like those Jesus observed giving at the temple, most of us give out of our abundance and really know nothing of giving sacrificially. He didn't condemn them for that, but He only commended the one who gave beyond what was reasonable.[65]

HAVE YOU EVER SACRIFICED FOR GOD?

Can you sacrifice for God? Is it even possible to do so?

When our family left the comfort of the US to move to Central America, my wife and I thought we were sacrificing. We particularly thought of all the things our children were going to miss, growing up outside the United States. But God gave back in so many ways that we realized it was anything but a sacrifice.

In fact, I've never been able to sacrifice for the Lord. I've tried. But every time I give something away or lay something down, He responds by giving back so much more–often in ways I never anticipated. Every time I give to the Lord, I come out ahead.

I've found all of God's blessings are like love–the more you give it away, the more it comes back to you, and the more you possess. Perhaps He's asking you to love more, to trust more, to take a walk on the waves and see what He will do as you leave your cage of comfort and begin to sacrificially store even more treasure in heaven.

There are thousands of places you could invest your money. We're honored and grateful you choose to invest in Commission To Every Nation. We see that investment as a sacred trust.

The value of your partnership can't even be estimated this side of eternity. Your giving makes it possible for your missionary friends to go. But you've been promised that when you sow you will also reap.

Our lavishly generous God has designed it so that you will share in the reward of the missionary's work.[66]

Don't be afraid to trust Him. Don't be afraid to obey Him. Don't hold back in the safety of the boat if God is inviting you to join Him in walking on the waves of His miraculous power. He is the God who is able to make you stand.

WHY WOULD ANYONE ABANDON A PERFECTLY GOOD BOAT?

Finally, this book is especially for you if you've been told all the reasons you aren't qualified, you can't do it, you should stay home, stay in the boat, stay with the other disciples, play it safe because you don't have what it takes. After all, you aren't some spiritual superstar. You're just an ordinary person.

You see, I believe He has a place for you in His continuing story. It's my hope that this book will challenge you to find that place and go after it with the assurance that God can and wants to use you. Anyone can be a missionary, or do whatever God has put in their heart, because it isn't about their qualifications. It's about His.

But good people who care about you—family and friends—are often the first to discourage you. They can't understand why anyone would jump out of a perfectly good boat and step into a tempest. They can't help but wonder why you would raise your own support, leave home, family, and the familiar, to go to a place that's dangerous, foreign, and sometimes doesn't even want you, your message, or your strange God.

These friends want the best for you, and they aren't doing anything wrong by staying in the boat themselves. That's where they belong. But like Peter, you've heard an invitation. You've been invited by the Lord himself to join Him in the storm. To carry his message and bless the nations.

Those who say you aren't qualified are absolutely right. That's one reason God pointed His finger at you. This way, when great things are accomplished, no one will have any doubt as to Who deserves the credit.

It is a crazy idea. Things could go wrong. It could cost you financially. It could ruin your reputation. It could destroy your career plans.

Jesus said you'll be like a sheep among wolves.[67] Wolves love sheep–for dinner. You could get hurt. Your family could get hurt. Let's face it, you could even die.

In fact, you will die. We all do. The only real question is, "Will you live before you die?" Will you choose to abandon the safety of the boat and risk obedience?

There's security in the boat. There's camaraderie in the boat. No one will question your sanity or criticize you for clinging to the boat. That's what smart people do when caught in a storm at sea.

But there are always a few crazy folks who "aren't very smart but can work hard." They refuse to live confined in comfort or enslaved to false security because they've heard the Lord's invitation. Like Peter, they recklessly respond.

It's not an invitation to think about it, ponder, and consider all the possibilities. Because no one can imagine all the possibilities. No one can predict what God's going to do in response to you taking that step of obedience. You'll never know until you step out.

You've heard an invitation to "Come." Obedience doesn't mean everything will go smoothly. Peter got overwhelmed and became terrified. But when he cried out, the Lord rescued him and enabled him to stand. He could have stayed in the boat, followed the conventional wisdom, and stayed dry. But Peter walked on water. Let that sink in for a moment. He Walked... On... Water. WOW!

In the midst of the storm, with the wind and waves crashing around him, an ordinary man overcame Analysis Paralysis. He didn't let Preparation Paralysis hold him back. Instead, he followed an insane invitation from his Lord. He left safety and security, stepped out and did the extraordinary. When it got rough, when he was about to go under, he cried out in terror and the Lord lifted him up and enabled him to stand.

WHICH VOICE WILL YOU FOLLOW?

Other disciples can stay in the boat. But you've heard His call. You've heard His invitation to join Him on the waves. So, it's time to decide. Do you listen to those who say that sane people don't leave career, family, friends, and security to step into a maelstrom of uncertainty?

Do you listen to your own fears? You might drown. Why would anyone support you? What makes you think you have what it takes? You're just an ordinary person, not some missionary superstar.

Or do you listen to the gentle invitation you hear above the storm?

"Come, join Me. Let's go for a walk on the waves and bless the nations."

You are free to make your choices
But keep in mind as you do
That once you make those choices
Those choices will make you.

– RICK MALM

■ ■ ■

Comfort zones are nice places but
nothing ever grows there.

– UNKNOWN

Why Send Missionaries?
The Four Most Common Questions

■ ■ ■

QUESTION ONE: WHY SEND MISSIONARIES WHEN THERE ARE SO MANY UNBELIEVERS AT HOME?

I'VE HAD WELL-MEANING PEOPLE SINCERELY ask me why we should send missionaries to other countries when there are so many lost people in our own neighborhoods. Here are three reasons we still need to invest in sending missionaries.

ACCESS

Sadly, it's true that there are millions of unbelievers in the United States and Canada, but there are also millions of believers in the US and Canada who can easily tell them about the Lord. Furthermore, a person in the US or Canada can hear the news of Jesus through 24/7 Christian radio, television, and online. We have access to Christian bookstores, magazines, free Bibles in hotel rooms, and churches on nearly every corner. A seeker in the US or Canada can easily find the Truth.

But there are millions of people in the world who couldn't tell you anything about who Jesus is or what He did. And they have no one to tell them and no way to hear. It is estimated that in some areas of the world, there is only one Christian worker (a pastor, lay leader, missionary, etc.) for every one million people. These people have no way to hear the gospel unless someone from outside their world goes to them with the message.

To paraphrase Oswald Smith, the founder of The People's Church in Toronto, Canada, "How can we justify allowing someone to hear and reject the gospel multiple times when there are so many who have never had the opportunity to hear it even once?"

WE DON'T HAVE TO CHOOSE

It's very true that we have many lost in our own neighborhoods, but it doesn't cost a dime for Christians in America to reach their neighbors. We don't have to stop supporting overseas missions to reach them. We simply need to mobilize the church to be the church. We can reach our neighbors and still send missionaries to other nations. There's no reason to consider this an either/or decision.

OBEDIENCE

Jesus told us to go locally and to the ends of the earth. (Acts 1:8) He did not give us the liberty to pick one or the other. That should be all the reason we need to support missions "in Jerusalem, **and** in all Judea, **and** in Samaria **and** unto the uttermost part of the earth."

If the apostles had waited until all Jerusalem and Judea and Samaria had heard the gospel before they reached out to the ends of the earth it's quite possible that today neither you nor I would have had the opportunity to know Jesus.

Because he came for all, we must go to all.

'Everyone who calls on the name of the Lord will
be saved.' How, then, can they call on the one they
have not believed in? And how can they believe in
the one of whom they have not heard? And how can
they hear without someone preaching to them? And
how can anyone preach unless they are sent?

- ROMANS 10:13-15

■ ■ ■

All authority in heaven and on earth has been given to
me. Therefore go and make disciples of all nations..."

- MATTHEW 28:18-19

QUESTION TWO: WHY SEND MISSIONARIES WHEN NATIONALS CAN DO IT CHEAPER AND BETTER?

Tomas is a respected leader among his Mayan people. A former mayor and now converted Christian, his people trust him. He understands the culture and speaks several Mayan languages as well as Spanish. Though only 5 feet tall, he is a spiritual giant. He fearlessly and repeatedly risked his life and led his people during the brutal civil war that devastated his land. He and his family live simply, and for just a few dollars of support a month, we can send him to minister full time to the Ixil people in the mountains of Northern Guatemala.

Examples like this lead some to ask, "Why send North American missionaries when the nationals can do it?" It's a logical question, especially when the resources available for missions seem so limited, and the need so unlimited. It's cheaper. They already speak the language. There are no cultural barriers. They cannot be deported if the political tide turns against Christian missionaries. Perhaps the day of sending North American missionaries is over, and we should just support national workers.

I SUPPORT SUPPORTING NATIONALS

I'm believe in helping men such as my friend, Tomas, but I'm also concerned that a narrow "either/or attitude" is more a plot than a plan–a plot to undermine and slow the work of world evangelism. Our options are not, "either support nationals or send missionaries." The task is so big we must do both. Here are some reasons why.

IS IT CHEAPER?

Often, but not always, it is cheaper to support national workers. They require less preparation because it is their own language and culture and they usually can live more simply in their home country. Let's face it, Christians love bargains. Sending money instead of sending people is absolutely easier. It requires little sacrifice. It does not mess with our comfort zones.

Like a country that hires mercenaries to battle for them, we can stay home, enjoying our comfy couches and the luxuries of life, all while paying others to shed the tears and spill their sweat and blood. I will send $20 or $200 or $2000. I will send whatever it costs, as long as I don't have to send my own sons and daughters, my own flesh and blood—as long as I don't have to sacrifice self or lose my lifestyle.

But God Himself set the example. The Greatest Missionary of all, Jesus, left the comforts of Heaven to come to us, to walk among the filth and mire of humanity. He did not send angels to do His bidding. He came in flesh to reveal the message of God's tender mercy. We dare not simply send others. Because He came for all, we must go to all.

CHEAPER IS NOT ALWAYS BETTER

"If it sounds too good to be true, it probably is." "You get what you pay for." These maxims are often as true in missions as they are in other areas of life. Cheaper does not always mean better. Just being from a country does not automatically mean you have the skills, calling or heart necessary for effective ministry in that country. Like North American ministers, there are some effective and there are some not-so-effective national workers. And it's hard to tell the difference from long distance.

It's easy to create reports, videos, and even onsite visits that make "not-so-effective" appear awesome. Stories abound of ineffective national workers who simply took advantage of their North American donors' generosity and naiveté. It is impossible to accurately evaluate what is really happening if you do not have culturally astute people onsite with insight. Cheaper *is* cheaper – but not always better.

THE NEED IS SO GREAT

In some nations, there are not enough national workers to accomplish the task without outside help. Imagine a country where there are only five Christians for every 100,000 people—and those five might live scattered across the map, and have very limited understanding of their faith. Without outside reinforcements, a handful of believers cannot reach their nation regardless of the amount of financial resources we might pump into their coffers.

God Has Given A Powerful Platform

Foreigners often have a "platform" that locals do not. My Spanish teacher lamented how he repeatedly had shared the gospel with people he knew, and they would not listen. Then a "gringo" with horrid Spanish would stumble through a gospel presentation and his friends would accept Jesus.

A Kachiquel Mayan man I met told how he came to the Lord because a group of white people visited his remote village. Even as a boy he thought, "Why would these rich, white people come to my poor village? What they have must be very important for them to come all this way to give it us." He listened and believed.

As North Americans, we're going to give account for how we use this platform the Lord has given us. Hollywood, Nashville and Madison Avenue marketers have taken advantage of it to spread our movies, music, materialism and debauchery around the world. Surely the message of the church needs to be proclaimed as loudly from this platform of privilege while it still exists in at least some countries.

People Are People

An influx of foreign money to support some national workers can create jealousy and undermine volunteerism in the local church. It can imply that you should be paid (and paid well) to do ministry. You're right, "Christians shouldn't feel this way," but people are people, no matter what country they're from.

Imagine if you're teaching Sunday School and discover that 10 other teachers are getting paid $400 a week for teaching but the pastor makes you buy your own chalk. Most of us would have a problem with that. We might think, "Maybe I'm not good enough," or "Maybe I'm not really wanted," or "This isn't fair," or even "Why should I continue to sacrifice time with my family and a better secular income when I'm not appreciated or wanted anyway?"

His Ways Are Not Our Ways

Have you noticed God frequently doesn't do what seems logical to us? In Scripture, He often calls the most unlikely candidates and seems unconcerned with the cost or efficiency of His chosen methods.

By our standards He frequently doesn't seem to be a good steward of His resources. Jesus allowed Judas to remain as treasurer even though He certainly knew Judas was stealing. He never even confronted him about it.

Saul was chastised for not destroying all the livestock of the Amalekites. But wasn't Saul simply being a "good steward," doing what seemed logical instead of following God's directives?

The Lord has not revised or revoked His command to "Go into all the world." We dare not follow the example of Saul and try to improve on God's plan because it makes better financial sense to us. Money is not a problem for God—but disobedience is.

Obviously I am not saying we are to be wasteful or squander His resources, but we must never forget they are *His* resources, not ours. Because they are His, we need to follow His directives on how they are spent, even if His plan does not seem the most efficient or cost effective to us.

Conclusion

Obedience is still God's measure for success, and the great commission command to "Go" is still in His Word. The task is so big we need "all hands on deck." We must continue to send foreign workers, national workers, and all who will respond to His call. While the harvest is still white and the laborers still few, I cannot say to one who senses God's call to go, "Sorry, I can't help you because you are not from there."

Question Three: Why Send Missionaries Into "Reached" Nations?

It was painful news. I wanted to give some words of encouragement but there was nothing helpful to say.

A brokenhearted missionary couple had just told me their home church would no longer financially support their ministry because the Missions Board decided they were only going to support missionaries going to unreached people groups (UPGs).

The pain wasn't just about the funds–although that obviously hurt too. But the church where they worshipped, fellowshipped, laughed and loved, the church that sent them to the mission field, was now saying the ministry they were giving their lives to was no longer valid, no longer needed, at least not worth supporting financially. Their home church could no longer "waste" missions money on them. Really?

What Is An Unreached People Groups?

A UPG is a group without enough Christians to evangelize the rest of the people in the group. This group will only be reached by sending outside reinforcements to aid the national Christians. No one disputes the crucial need for sending missionaries to these areas, but here are some problems I see with choosing to only support missionaries to UPGs.

It's About Discipleship

Certainly we need to encourage more work among unreached people. But the command of Jesus was not just to reach people, not just to make converts. He said make disciples. That means reaching people is not enough. We can't just go; we must also be prepared to stay. Making disciples is not a "been there, done that, check the box, let's move on" project.

Making disciples takes time. It means forming trusting relationships. It's not as glamorous. It doesn't lend itself to measurable statistics or great photo ops. It certainly isn't as exciting as "going where no Christian has gone before," but it is what we were told to do.

It's About Obedience

I joined the military during wartime. I requested overseas duty but was assigned stateside. Surely the needs were greater over there–in the combat zone. But if I disregarded my orders and went to the front lines because I decided the need was greater there, I could have been court martialed for desertion. Soldiers must report for duty where they're assigned.

Are all missionaries working in "reached" areas mistaken about where God assigned them? Did He really call them to go to a UPG, but they misunderstood or rejected that call to go to where they wanted to go? Do I dare make that judgment?

It's About People

Some might ask, "If a church wants to support missionaries to UPGs couldn't their current missionaries simply relocate to where UPGs are?"

Sure they could but …

Missionaries and their families aren't inanimate pawns on a chess board that we can casually move from square to square whenever we get excited about a new strategy. Often they have served for years, building trust and effective ministries in one area or among one group of people. Learning the subtleties of a language, discovering keys to the culture and earning a hearing among a group of people can take decades. Moving means abandoning years of invested time, talent, and treasure and frankly, can mean going where they may feel no calling to serve.

Why The Double Standard?

Obviously the US and Canada are reached countries. Should we no longer send missionaries to North American campuses? Should we no longer have missionaries working among the military or in urban slums, among the homeless and those enslaved in prostitution? Should we not support those fighting to stop the holocaust of abortion or human trafficking because the US and Canada are "reached" nations?

If it's legitimate to support ministries that battle these crucial areas of great darkness in our own country, then how can we say it's not legitimate to support those who battle the same forces of darkness in other "reached" nations?

WHERE IS REALLY "REACHED"?

Should we stop supporting missionaries in the Philippines, Europe, Latin America, parts of Africa and Asia, or even North America because there are too many Christians in those countries?

Should missionaries abandon their work caring for orphans and widows, refugees and the outcast? Should they stop fighting human trafficking, salvaging discarded and abused women and children, caring for victims of war and violence, victims of disease, disintegrating family structures, and other fruits of sin and lost humanity, because the population has reached some randomly determined percentage of Christians?

IS THERE NOT A CAUSE?

There is a need for missionaries to UPGs, but there is still a need for those who, like Aaron and Hur, will come alongside strong national leaders to hold up their arms, encourage and serve.[68] There are still astronomical needs in "reached" nations that require us to continue to send those who God has called to those nations.

Trends come and go in missions, as they do in our secular society. But wisdom requires we not abandon all that has been done to this point to run after the latest fad. Instead, we must stay the course, follow the Lord's directions, and continue to "go and make disciples of **all** nations."

The command is not to just make converts among those who have never heard. It is to make disciples of all nations.

QUESTION FOUR: WHY SEND MISSIONARIES WHEN THEY DESTROY NATIVE CULTURES?

Repeat a lie often enough, and it will become a well-known fact. One such "fact" is that missionaries destroy local cultures. Obviously, missionaries make mistakes, and some have exported their own culture thinking it was Biblical culture. But let me share a story that offers another perspective.

I had just finished working with a medical/dental team for two weeks in the mountain highlands of Guatemala, Central America. On the way back to Guatemala City we stopped at one of the most gorgeous spots on Earth–Lake Atitlan. We crossed the lake by boat to visit some villages so the doctors could have a little break from the grueling schedule of the last two weeks.

I was walking with one of the doctors when we came across a woman, an indigenous Tzutujil Mayan, working under a tree beside the wide walking path we were following. A handmade fence of sticks, approximately 4 feet high, separated us and outlined her family's small patch of dirt next to the trail. A one-room adobe home, complete with dirt floor, stood in one corner of the plot of land, and she sat in a corner close to the path. She was dressed in the colorful blouse and skirt of her tribe, though the colors were muted by dust and age. She sat in the dirt, weaving with a backstrap loom that is common in that area. We stopped for a moment to admire her artistry and the postcard scene.

She was probably only in her forties, but a hard life gave her the appearance of a very weathered seventy year old. I told the doctor she would work on this piece for weeks or even months and then only make a few dollars for her labors. She probably had several children to care for and had likely lost one or two to disease, poor nutrition, or lack of prenatal care. If her husband was still with her, he might be hours away on the coast working in the cane fields, or he might be a drunkard who only comes home to rape her and take any money he can find. Village life is hard.

After a few moments another "turista" stopped and struck up a conversation. He said he was from Israel and asked what we were doing in Guatemala. The doctor answered, "I'm a medical missionary."

I Like The "Medical" Part

Our new friend responded, "I like the 'medical' part but I don't think I like the 'missionary' part. Missionaries destroy the native culture of the people."

My doctor friend calmly responded, "Just what part of their culture are you so concerned about preserving? Is it the part where a man routinely gets drunk and beats his wife? Or the part that treats women like beasts of burden? Or the part that forbids girls from getting an education that could help them escape their poverty? Or how about the part where most women cook over an open fire in a small room so their lungs are so full of smoke..."

Our new friend had turned and walked away. I think he was offended. But the doctor was being much kinder than I would have been.

After living and working with the Mayan people, the politically correct attitude of this tourist became reprehensible to me. It treats indigenous people as props in colorful photo ops, as animals in a living zoo that should be maintained "as is" for our viewing pleasure.

Those who promote the glorious virtues of the native cultures do not identify with the people enough to even see them as real human beings. What makes me say something so judgmental about their concerns for preserving the culture?

The Crucial Question

I always want to ask, "If that was your mother sitting in the dirt, facing the hardships of daily life that this poor woman faces, would you be so committed to maintaining her culture or would you do something, whatever you could, to give her a better life?

Could you snap a photo and walk away, muttering about how beautiful her life is, if that was your daughter and you knew there was a high probability of her being raped and pregnant by age 16? Would your primary concern be cultural preservation if it was your sister and you knew her lack of education and opportunity would result in her remaining trapped in poverty, sleeping in the dirt, with no access to medical or dental care and no hope of a brighter future?

Would you encourage her to continue cooking in a tiny room over an open fire knowing that this quaint aspect of her culture produces over exposure to carbon dioxide producing respiratory illnesses and harming her children—both those already born and those in her womb?

If you wouldn't celebrate a culture that would do these things to your mother or daughter or sister, how can you think it's virtuous to insist this poor woman—or any human being – remain trapped in such wretchedness? Perhaps because it makes for great photos. Perhaps because it allows you to tell wonderfully interesting stories about how happy all the people are. "See how they're smiling in my photos with them."

People have told me "they get used to it," or "they don't know any better." First of all, when you get close enough to these people that they open up and share their heart – their hopes, dreams and fears – you realize that's nonsense.

How does a person "get used" to the constant ache of hunger, or watching their children's hair thin and fall out because of malnutrition? Do you think they get used to watching their children die from easily curable diseases—that it doesn't bother them because "they don't know any better?" It's only the outside "experts" who believe such nonsense.

It's not that they don't know any better. It's not that they get used to it. It's not that they're committed to preserving the chains of their indigenous culture. They have little option and the politically correct zookeeper mentality doesn't help them move toward a better life for them or their children. Let's keep them poor and sitting in the dirt so we can take home amazing, colorful pictures to show to our friends.

What Changes Do You Oppose?

Yes, missionaries change cultures. In India, widows are no longer burned to death or expected to commit suicide because their husband died. Endless revenge killings and cannibalism are no longer the norm among many jungle tribes. I've actually heard supercilious scholars mourn the loss of even these horrendous aspects of "culture." Unbelievable!

Missionaries have fought to change indigenous cultures that practice female mutilation (wrongly called female circumcision), human sacrifice, and enslaving of conquered tribes. They've fought to save the lives and dignity of handicapped children that are discarded as cursed by many cultures.

They seek to free people from alcoholism and drug addiction that tears apart families and the very fabric of societies. They work to put an end to human trafficking, sex slavery, treating women like property and treating children like slaves required to work while being denied an education.

Do You Really Believe They Do It Alone?

But what thinking person believes a missionary can change a culture if the people don't see some personal benefit to the change? A missionary can't just say, "Do it this way," and have an entire group of people mindlessly obey. Like all of us, people change when they experience benefit to themselves and their family. Otherwise they don't.

Practice What You Preach

Finally, if you apply this "preserve the culture" philosophy to our own country, Henry Ford, Thomas Edison, and many human rights warriors go from hero to villain. Our culture has certainly changed.

Unless you're Amish, you no longer depend on horses and buggies for transportation. Children no longer work sunup to sundown in coal mines or factories. Women can vote and no longer wash hand-made clothes with a scrub board. Slavery is illegal and education for children is mandatory.

For those who believe preserving native cultures is such a lofty goal, I suggest they try it at home first before they sell it to others. Let them get rid of their cell phones, laptops and televisions that have so dramatically changed our culture. Let them go back to the roots of their culture and their ancestors' lifestyles. Then, if they discover horses are better than cars, candles are better than electric lights, bloodletting beats penicillin, hunting is better than a supermarket, sleeping in dirt is better than their plush beds, etc., etc. Then they can authoritatively stand up and proclaim the glory of preserving native cultures.

CHANGE IS INEVITABLE

With or without missionary involvement, cultures are going to change. Rather than destroying cultures, missionaries have often guided the change in positive ways that protected vulnerable populations from those who would only exploit them.

Missionaries have been the ones who do the most to preserve the positive aspects of native cultures–often spending an entire lifetime learning a language, creating an alphabet, and then producing written records of rich tribal stories and traditions so the language and culture can be preserved.

When we see native people as real human beings with value equal to ours rather than props in a photo op, compassion will compel us to do all we can to help them improve their condition. But remember, people will only adopt cultural changes that prove beneficial to them. They'll reject ones that aren't. Ultimately it's up to them to preserve or change their culture.

For another look at this question from an established missionary/statesman, check out: *Do Missionaries Destroy Cultures?* by Don Richardson

http://bit.ly/2g0WKpg

Speech by Gladys Aylward

■ ■ ■

GLADYS AYLWARD WAS A BRITISH missionary to China before and during World War II. The film, *The Inn of the Sixth Happiness*, is based on her work but presents a highly fictionalized account. The book, *The Small Woman*, by Alan Burgess, presents a more accurate picture of her life and ministry.

This transcript comes from a recording sometime after her return to Britain in 1948. She tried to return to China in 1958 but was denied entry so she settled in Taiwan where she died in 1970 at age 67.

I include this transcript for a number of reasons.

1. She is a marvelous example of an ordinary, "unqualified" person who made herself available and saw God do amazing things through her.
2. It illustrates her lack of training, skills, and even prior study of the country and culture to which the Lord was calling her. While there's no reason to applaud such ignorance, it also shows that if we are going to be effective, we have to remember

it's because "God is able," not because of our study, strategies, or skills.

3. She poignantly shares some of the painful obstacles she had to overcome, including outright discouragement from her own family. Her story might encourage others facing similar barriers.

4. Perhaps the biggest reason I included this transcript is because it's my dream that when future Gladys Aylwards feel God saying, "Go," they won't face additional obstacles from agencies and people that should be helping them. Instead, my dream is that they'll find CTEN, and a host of others, cheering them on, encouraging and helping them fulfill the dream of the Lord for them and the people He is sending them to.

Her Speech

"When I went to China I had never seen a Chinese person. I didn't even know where China was. To me it was just a black dot on the map somewhere. And I'm afraid I had a terrific shock when I got there to find how large it was. I only knew that little, green island of England, and now before me stretched that great, huge, wonderful and beautiful land with its teeming millions of aching and hungry hearts. I truly believe He asked me to go.

"You see one day He walked along and crossed my path and He said "come," and I went. And He said, 'You can't do anything, you know. I'll do it through you.'

"And I remember going home when I felt God was calling me to China and saying to my father, 'You know dad, I would like to go to China.' And my father, rather a silent sort of man, but pretty straight, and he sat there and said, 'And what do you think you are going to do?'

And I said, 'I don't know.'

'Well you're not a nurse are you?'

'No, no I'm not.'

'Well you can't nurse anybody.'

'No,' I said, 'no I can't.'

'And you can't teach anything can you?'

'No,' I said, 'I can't.'

"And then he suddenly swung around and looked at me and said, 'O God, get out,' he said, 'All you can do is talk.'

"And I remember turning back and going outside the kitchen door and standing in that little passage at the bottom of the stairs and having and... well... having a little weep. He didn't understand, bless him, because you see God hadn't called him. He had called me.

"And then, suddenly, in the middle of my tears. There came this: Well, isn't that it?

"And so standing there I said, 'O Lord, well, he said talk. Well all right then, I'll talk. And I'll talk and I'll talk and I'll talk and I'll talk and I'll just keep on talking but it will be for you.'

"Nobody, least of all my dear father, dreamed of how true his words were going to become. Almost from that very moment God put words into my mouth and I've talked solidly ever since."[69]

Images

■ ■ ■

T.E.A.M. Missions Logo (1994 -1999)

Richard Malm

Commission
<u>TO EVERY NATION</u>

Original CTEN Logo (1999-2010)

Second CTEN logo adopted in November 2010

CTEN Canada Logo

Commission To Every Nation Offices in Texas

Commission To Every Nation Staff 1999

Back Row: Rick Malm; Scott Walston, Associate Director; Buddy Slate, Facilities Care; Joyce Slate, Bookkeeping
Front Row: Jana Malm; Jonathan Malm, IT/Web; Charlsie Cawthon, Publications

STATE OF TEXAS
OFFICE OF THE GOVERNOR

GEORGE W. BUSH
GOVERNOR

October 18, 1999

Greetings to:

Commission To Every Nation

Congratulations on your fifth anniversary. The October 23-24 open house and dedication ceremony provide great opportunities for Kerrville residents and supporters to tour your new facilities and celebrate your accomplishments as an interdenominational missions organization.

Texas has a strong spiritual foundation. Organizations such as yours provide a place where people can enjoy Christian fellowship, learn more about missionary outreach opportunities and strengthen their faith. I commend your ministry of teaching, comforting and providing assistance to people around the world.

Laura joins me in sending best wishes on this special occasion.

Sincerely,

GEORGE W. BUSH

POST OFFICE BOX 12428 AUSTIN, TEXAS 78711 (512) 463-2000

Letter to Commission to Every Nation
from then Texas Governor George Bush
upon the dedication of our Texas Office.

Commission To Every Nation Staff 2017

Front Row (L-R): Jack and Carol Rothenflue, CTEN USA Director; Jana and Rick Malm, Founders and President; Jana and Trevor Eby, CTEN Canada Director

Row2: Birdie and Dick Johnson, Pastoral Care; Tammie and Stephen Burger, Pastoral Care; B and Bob Nesbitt, Pastoral Care; Sensitive Regions, Pastoral Care Row 3: David and Janice Ewing, Pastoral Care; Rob and Joany Wills, Pastoral Care; Rita Hall, Publications Assistant; Tess Polk, Publications Assistant; Debi Stamm, Publications Manager Row 4: Angie Newby, Comptroller; Trinette Zirkel, Finance Manager; Laura Lee, Donor Care; Sylvie Beveridge, Canada Donor Care; Donna Ellis, Donor Care; John Hauk, Canada Finance Manager; Marcia Wortman, Assistant to the President; Buddy Slate, Facilities Care; Sherri White, Executive Assistant to the US Director; Mariko and Heath Meikle, Canada Missions Catalyst

END NOTES

1. Ephesians 2:10 (NLT)

2. Hebrews 10:29

3. Ephesians 2:7

4. Psalm 103:14

5. Romans 13:11, 12 NLT; Luke 10:2

6. Ephesians 2:10

7. Acts 4:13

8. I Corinthians 1:27

9. 1 Samuel 22:2

10. 1 Samuel 9:2

11. Romans 14:4 NIV

12. John 3:30 NIV

13. Romans 14:4 NIV

14. Romans 14:4)

15. Ecclesiastes 10:10

16. Acts 4:13

17. 2 Peter 1:5 NIV

18. 1 Corinthians 2:1-2 NLT

19. James 4:6, 1 Peter 5:5

20. 2 Corinthians 4:17 NIV

21. Romans 10:14

22. Genesis 32

23. St. John of the Cross

24. Psalm 71:20 NLT

25. Luke 4:1,14

26. 2 Timothy 2:12; Romans 8:17; 1 Peter 4:13; James 1:2

27. Isaiah 53:3

28. James 1:2-4 NLT

29. Philippians 2:7

30. 1 Corinthians 4:13

31. 2 Corinthians 8:21 NIV

32. G. Campbell Morgan

33. 2 Corinthians 9:7 NIV

34. "The Strenuous Life" speech by Theodore Roosevelt, 1899

35. Mark 8:19, 20

36. Matthew 9:37

37. Mark 2:27 NLT

38. 1 Thessalonians 5:24, Romans 14:4

39. Luke 10:2 NLT

40. Matthew 10:42

41. Luke 22:35 NIV

42. 1 Corinthians 3:12

43. Philippians 4:12-13 NIV

44. Acts 12

45. William Carey (1761-1834), often referred to as "the father of modern missions", had to battle the prevailing attitude of his day that the great commission was just for the original disciples. Most churches were not interested in sending missionaries. He eventually formed a mission society that sent him to India.

46. Gladys Aylward (1902-1970) was turned down to be a missionary because of her age and lack of education. She was even cruelly told how unqualified she was by her own father (See addendum 2). She courageously overcame the opposition and became a highly-respected missionary to the Chinese people.

47. Acts 15:39

48. Acts 16:6-10

49. Acts 16 & 19

50. 2 Corinthians 11:27

51. Luke 6:38

52. Proverbs 19:17 NLT

53. 1 Corinthians 1:27, 28 NLT

54. Deuteronomy 7:9 NLT

55. Psalm 103:14

56. Proverbs 22:7 NIV

57. John 14:34

58. 2 Corinthians 1:8-9

59. Exodus 17:8-12

60. 1 Kings 17

61. Luke 16:12

62. James 4:8

63. Romans 8:28 NLT

64. Matthew 6:33

65. Mark 12:43

66. Matthew 10:41

67. Matthew 10:16

68. Exodus 17:12

69. Aylward speech available at https://youtu.be/3_xngUfIL6U

ABOUT THE AUTHOR

■ ■ ■

RICHARD MALM IS A PASTOR, missionary, Christian educator, parent, grandparent, and husband to Jana for over forty years. They have three grown children - Joel, Charis and Jonathan - all of whom married amazing spouses and have, thus far, given them three precious granddaughters.

He's often amazed when he realizes he's the founder of Commission To Every Nation (www.cten.org), an interdenominational mission organization that has enabled the ministry of thousands of missionaries around the globe.

He holds a bachelor's degree in business administration, a master's in educational administration and, in the unlikely event he decides to complete his dissertation, he'll receive a PhD in pastoral ministry.

His has written various magazine and newspaper articles plus published several books, all of which have been highly successful at eluding notice by the New York Times Bestseller list.

Rick lives in Kerrville, Texas where he likes feeding the birds and, to the irritation of some of his neighbors, the pesky deer.